The Solution

Executive

Transform Your Expertise

Into Impact

Kristen McAlister

Table of Contents

Preface

For more than 15 years, I have had the opportunity to be involved in hundreds of discussions with business owners, CEOs, investors, boards, and executives. I understand business challenges, the triggers causing the challenges, and the variety of solutions a company can deploy to resolve the issues. These range from how to scale a company to how to turn a company around. As an executive matchmaker, I understand how to align the various experiences and accomplishments in an executive's career with the challenges businesses experience. I understand what drives business decisions, and I understand what motivates executives when making career decisions.

It is from all these experiences that I can say with confidence: How we address solving business problems and building leadership teams needs to change.

I have become part therapist and part evangelist for business owners and leadership teams that are getting stuck, going down the wrong road, and can't figure out what to do next — as well as job seekers and independent executives who are frustrated and feel taken advantage of. There is a better way to align what people do best — and enjoy doing — with companies that need that expertise.

Figuring out what a business needs, how an executive can help that business, and aligning the two is easy neither for the business owner(s) nor for the executive looking to help. This ends up being the center of every conversation, whether it is with the business' leadership figuring out what they want to accomplish and what expertise is needed to do that, or with independent executives figuring out what they are best at and the types of business situations they enjoy helping. I woke up one morning a few months ago, and everything inside me said, "It is time to make aligning the two easier for everyone involved."

With the evolution of independent executives and the abundance of executives available to help companies navigate these challenges, I want to provide some common language on how we help and what we are looking to accomplish. The concepts are not new, but *how* these concepts are applied to each of us individually to help find and communicate how we help businesses grow will bring some new thoughts to the discussion.

I realize that someone who has been a controller or CFO may not have been involved in creating a brand or building a go-to-market strategy. They may never even have done a client presentation. Conversely, some of us have done these for most of our careers but have not thought about how to apply these to ourselves and the careers we want.

Regardless of an executive's functional expertise and background, the same concepts that apply to building any business apply to creating the career you want. It starts with figuring out what you do best and enjoy doing, identifying who needs this, and creating a feedback loop to do it on repeat until it is natural to you. Good news: The market opportunity is there, and the market size is every company in the world.

There is more opportunity to help companies than ever before and more need for it. However, just as we would advise any business, change is constant. The economic challenges have changed, how we buy has changed, the businesses we serve have been forced to change and evolve, and so must we change and evolve how we find, communicate, and work with them. It isn't about us; it's about them and how we can help, one way or another.

The more intentional we are about our expertise and how we can help with the ever-changing landscape of business, and the easier it is to align these two and connect the dots, the easier it will be for us all to get to where we want to be.

CHAPTER 1

Story of an Executive Career

If it were 30 years ago, this would be a very short book. You'd go to college, work with a company for 30–40 years, and retire. End of story.

If that were truly the end of the story, then I wouldn't have had the opportunity to meet thousands of executives over the years who have had a very different story — some intentionally, most accidentally.

We are all familiar with the traditional career, where you work for one or more companies for a set number of years. You then retire, collect your pension and other sources of income, and enjoy whatever mix of activities you like. For executives, this has become the exception rather than the rule. The concept, and possibly the definition, of retirement has changed. Even my father, who graduated with a master's degree in electrical engineering and stayed with the same company his entire first career (note the word *first*), didn't choose this track. During his initial retirement, he did something that shocked us all. After six months of his retirement, my mom did a bit of research and found a need for electrical engineers at utilities in the Southwest. After some further research and legwork, he was on contract. He then spent the next couple of decades moving around and picking up contracts with various other utilities. My father did not go to business school and was never an executive. He had a niche skill set, found a market need for it, and put it out for sale. He eventually productized it and generated multiple revenue streams. Anyone who knows my father drops their jaw when they hear the story. It was so unlike him. My father spent 30 years waking up at the same time every morning, going to work, and coming home at the end of the day. Yet he chose to leverage his skills into contract roles after close to 30 years in the same career with the same company in the utilities industry. He wasn't ready to retire, he knew the world still has a use for what he did, and he figured out a way to continue to work on his terms.

I have seen executive careers take many forms over the past couple of decades. Executives have more options than ever when making their next career choice: taking a full-time position, retiring, board work, being independent as a contract executive, or a combination of these.

I get the opportunity to work with a variety of executives, helping them figure out their next career choice and how to align it with what businesses need. One of the most common executive personas that will help me share various stories and explain concepts is Ethan. Ethan has had some successes in his career. He spent almost 30 years working in companies from startups to Fortune 100. He has worked with companies that are family-owned, founder-led, and private equity–owned through acquisition. The most recent acquisition led to a new CEO and ownership who brought in their own leadership team. Having been through a range of intense experiences drawing on a variety of skills, Ethan was ready to do something different. He didn't want to join another company and roll the dice on how long that would go and not have any control over what would happen to that role.

Ethan represents tens of thousands of executives:

- The finance executive who came up through public accounting into a controller role. They worked their way into a CFO role, gaining additional experience with a couple of small acquisitions in the process. The owner eventually sold to a large competitor in the industry.
- The operations executive who has spent most of their career growing manufacturing or service-delivery systems for various companies, moving from one location to the next each time the company decided to move, the division sold, or they wanted the next challenge and moved on voluntarily.
- The marketing executive with a career in Fortune 500 brands. The company they worked for decided to reduce their investment in marketing efforts and consolidated all marketing spend to a small team at corporate outside the U.S. and outsourced the rest.
- The IT executive who started their career as a developer. They had the opportunity to spend time inside business units as an IT partner and understand how business works. They have been through a couple of acquisitions integrating companies with multiple platforms into one succinct system. After working with two startups with the hope of being on the ground floor, neither worked out.

- The business owner who spent 20 years growing a business and eventually sold it. They made every mistake possible and could write a book on the lessons learned. They aren't ready to retire and don't want to build another business themselves, but they still want to be involved in a business.

- The corporate development executive who spent most of their career acquiring and integrating companies. They know everything there is to know about how to identify a potential deal, go through due diligence, and execute the initial 100-day plan. The company has decided to hold off on any more acquisitions and has laid off most of the corporate development division. The new CEO wants to grow with a different vision.

- The human resources leader who has spent their career working with different cultures, understands how to engage employees, and has been responsible for thousands of employees all over the world. There isn't an employee situation they haven't seen and solved. The current company has decided to restructure, and the HR leader's position is eliminated.

- The sales executive who has built, rebuilt, and scaled sales divisions in a variety of companies and industries. They understand how a customer buys, how to position the product to solve a pain in the marketplace, how to identify talent, and how to create a repeatable sales process. The industry hit a downturn, and regardless of the external environment, the CEO thinks a new/fresh perspective in sales leadership will make the difference.

What's next?

They all have great resumés with companies, titles, and experiences. They each want more flexibility in their schedule, control over whom they work with, or to do more of the work they enjoy.

And so they say, "Let's transition to being an independent executive."

Great news: There is more opportunity than ever ...

CHAPTER 2

What's a Company to Do?

The traditional model of options for a growing company involved filling out an organization chart that aligned with their budget and their philosophies. A business owner had a leadership team made up of the first couple of people they hired who have been elevated beyond their skill sets or a new executive hire from outside the company. They are very excited about the new hire. The interviews were like having a conversation with an old friend, the executive has worked with some large companies, and they have incredible accomplishments. If they have done all that in their career, this company and what it wants them to do is a walk in the park. Fast forward to 12 months later: A lot of money has been spent, the company is no closer to their goal, and the business owner and executive part ways, frustrated.

Like executives who experience these frustrations and know there has to be a better way, business owners have discovered a new option for growing their companies and solving their problems: the independent executive model.

When an executive gives notice, it used to take a couple of weeks to figure out what to do and for the suggestion and acceptance of the concept of an interim executive come into view. Bringing in an interim executive is now the first thought. If the board doesn't already know a firm or resource, it takes them 2–3 days to find one, and an interim is sitting in the seat within 1–2 weeks of the initial departure notice. Companies and leadership teams understand the concept of bringing in an interim executive to fill a gap while a search for the longer-term individual is conducted. It is also commonplace for a growing company to have at least one leadership role be a fractional executive.

Companies are using the independent executive model to test roles and concepts. It has gone from a way to fill a departure to a way to be innovative. I was recently watching a CEO present his company organizational chart. Next to the chief operating officer and chief human resources officer was the interim chief transformation officer. Transformation, by virtue of its name, tends to be temporary and not a role a small to mid-size company needs longer term. It makes a lot of sense, once it is discussed, and these discussions are now multiplying.

I started seeing interim chief revenue officers several years ago. As companies reorganize to consolidate the accountability of the top line to one person, it is now a common role for companies. Next was interim vice president of sales operations, as companies needed to bridge the gap between sales and operations for the sake of their bottom line. More recently, interim chief of staff is being used to create a right-hand internal advisor, facilitator, and driver of initiatives on behalf of the CEO or president.

CHAPTER 3

Leverage the Opportunity: From Education to Differentiation

It used to be that executives such as Ethan would transition to being independent, hang a solopreneur shingle, and start networking. Ethan would leverage an impeccable resumé with some great logos and accomplishments on it, and he'd know that after a few phone calls, he'd be set up and working on his first interim assignment. But now the reality, after six months, is that Ethan has done a couple of small projects and given a lot of free advice. He is asking himself why: "What happened? Why do I not have companies lined up at my door wanting me to help them?"

More adoption brings more opportunities, and more opportunities bring more competition. When I am asked, "Whom do you see as your competitors," my answer has always been, "Anyone who can solve a business' problem." I do not see independent executives as filling a contract executive need; I see them as a vehicle to solving a business problem. The increased accessibility to various means of solving a business problem is driving more segmentation in the marketplace — and the need for clarity and differentiation.

With the increased popularity of the independent executive option, the concept of being an independent executive has evolved from explaining what an interim or fractional executive is, to explaining why they are better than the 10 other interim or fractional executives. We have moved from education to differentiation. Businesses now have multiple readily available options to consider when working with an independent executive. This is driving the increased importance of segmentation and differentiation.

What do you do when you can offer a lot of value but have a lot of competition?

Find the pain, and be the solution!

The biggest challenge we face is: How do we apply our experience and skill set to help solve company problems?

Answering this may seem daunting. Don't worry, I'll show you how.

We can make it easy.

Make it easy for people to understand what problems you solve and how you help companies.

Make it easy for people to remember you.

Make it easy for prospective clients to trust that you can solve their problem.

Make it easy for them to take the chance and move forward on your solution for their situation.

Remember, they have the option to move forward with anyone who can solve their problem. You also have the option to decide what you want to do, what problems you want to solve, whom you want to work with, and whether you want to say "yes" or "no" to the opportunity to work with them. To do this, like anything else, we need a plan.

CHAPTER 4

The Independent Executive Business Plan

Whichever career path you choose, there is as much value in creating a plan as there is for any business. Let's look at two very similar businesses: one with a plan and one without a plan.

Imagine meeting a business owner, Roger, who is struggling with his business and can't figure out why. You start asking questions. As the questions and answers unfold, Roger shares that he started making cheesecakes for friends and family a few years ago. It was a family recipe he has fine-tuned over the years. Anyone who eats a piece of his cheesecake says it is the best they have ever had. One day, Roger strikes up a conversation with a local restaurant manager who is intrigued and wants to try the cheesecake. After a taste test, the manager orders five to sell at the restaurant. Roger adds up his cost of ingredients, some compensation for the time it takes him to bake them, puts a little extra on it for drive time, and gives a price of $25 per cheesecake. This continued with a few more restaurants and local stores. Three years later, Roger has never worked so hard in his life, been so stressed, and made so little money.

Roger doesn't have a business plan (written or otherwise). He's never really thought it through. He's making $10 on every cheesecake and can make 10 of them at a time in about an hour. In his mind, he is making $100 per hour, which is not bad. His go-to-market plan is word of mouth and chatting up restaurants and local store owners in the area. To him, these are all the paths of least resistance and come naturally to him.

Conversely, I know someone who recently did start a cheesecake business. This is the fourth business she has started, with a successful exit of her first, and the other two are concurrent with the cheesecake business. She has a business plan, she has done her market research, she knows what other cheesecakes like hers sell for ($60–$80 each), and every minute she puts into the business is intentional. This is partly because it is who she is, and partly because any minute she spends on the cheesecake business takes away from the other two businesses and the income-producing activities she could be doing.

Think of your efforts as an independent executive in terms of a business you are starting. Like my friend who started her cheesecake business, consider every minute or hour you put into it as time being taken from something else, whether it is revenue-generating opportunities, your friends and family, or self-care (you) time.

Your executive career is your cumulative experience being leveraged to have a successful business, and it starts with a business plan. It is a plan for how to market and sell your experience, your skill sets, and the problems you can solve. Even if you are a well-known business author and consultant, such as Jim Collins, whose name is a brand and can sell itself, the brand represents his experience, his knowledge, and the hurdles he has helped so many of us get past through his writings, consulting, etc. You are selling what you can do for a client. When a client engages your services, there is an agreement between you and the client that includes a statement of work. The statement of work does not list your resumé. It lists the engagement goals, what problems exist, what will be done, expected outcomes, and deliverables.

We'll explore the possibilities of building the independent executive career you want and creating a fluid, ongoing stream of opportunities, whether you remain independent or do something else. I challenge you to explore yourself and your career — and be authentic about where you are and where you want to go.

Here's a preview of the journey we'll go on together:

- **Your Why**: Why do you want to be independent, why you are choosing one independent option over another, what is driving you?
- **Your executive brand**: What are you great at, what is the value you bring, what problems do you solve?
- **Potential clients**: Who has the problems you solve?
- **Go-to-market**: How do you find companies/individuals with the problems you solve and connect with them? I'll give a range of strategies to think through or help jumpstart your thoughts on what works for you.
- **Alignment**: Understand what a company needs, and decide if you are the right solution or not. We'll go through the discovery process and analyze what a company actually needs. The purpose is more for you than for the company. This is your opportunity to decide if the situation makes sense for you to say "yes" or "not for me, here's another resource."

- **Getting to "yes"**: Once you decide it is right for you, how do you make it easy for the client to say "yes," as well? We'll explore possibilities for productizing what you do, what you should charge, and reducing the risk for everyone involved to move forward.

Let's go build your business!

Pulling It All Together

1. The concept, and possibly the definition, of retirement has changed.

2. Executives have more options than ever when making their next career choice: taking a full-time position, retiring, board work, being independent as a contract executive, or a combination of these.

3. Companies and leadership teams understand the concept of bringing in an interim executive to fill a gap while a search for a longer-term individual is conducted. It is also commonplace for a growing company to have at least one leadership role be a fractional executive.

4. Companies are using the independent executive model to test roles and concepts.

5. More adoption brings more opportunities, and more opportunities bring more competition.

6. The increased accessibility to various means of solving a business problem is driving increased segmentation in the marketplace — and the need for clarity and differentiation.

7. Find the pain, and be the solution!

8. Build an independent executive business plan as you would for any other revenue-generating activity.

CHAPTER 5

Find Your Why

The modern executive career is full of changes that cause zigs and zags in the road. It is rarely a straight path. While the events prompting the change may not be within their control, what the executive does next is within their control. Part of that decision-making is determined by their "Why."

Why are you choosing this path (contract, direct hire, other)?

- I want to help companies to not make the same mistakes I did.
- I enjoy M&A deals and want to do more of them.
- I need a full-time, ongoing, stable income.
- I want to get a CEO role or exit on my resumé.
- I want to find the next company to help grow and exit.
- I want or need more flexibility in my schedule.
- My spouse says the house is only big enough for one of us to be in it full time.

Most are ways an executive can work with and make an impact for companies and leaders. They can offer a great amount of flexibility, financial security, additional experience, and challenges. Getting clarity on why you are choosing one option over another will help you get there faster. A comment I get often is, "I am open to anything I can get." I understand we may be open to considering anything due to monetary circumstances. But I will challenge anyone making this statement to prioritize the potential options, think through their Why, and be more purposeful with their intentions. Get specific. Being specific will shorten the timeline greatly.

To figure out your Why, think back on your experiences, what you accomplished, what you enjoyed and didn't enjoy, what was driving you in each situation. Now align that with your current situation and what is driving you.

I like to use Bob as a good example for getting clarity on what drives and excites you. Bob spent much of his career growing a single company. About nine months after selling it, his friend Joe reached out for some help. Joe also owned a company, and he knew Bob had a knack for identifying bottlenecks, getting to the heart of a problem, and creating an empowering environment that gets everyone rowing in the same direction. After six months of bouncing ideas and problems off Bob, Joe asked him to come in and help solve a few issues. Next thing Bob knew, three years had gone by, and they were selling Joe's company. Bob realized he was good at this and that he loved helping Joe, though some parts were more fun for him than others. He did enjoy helping Joe decide where he wanted to take the company, get the right leadership team in place, and create the roadmap to a successful exit. He did not enjoy working 60 hours a week and managing a team on a daily basis. Bob could clearly see he wanted to help small-business owners figure out how to solve problems and build an infrastructure that could scale and be sold. Bob has had two successful exits and enjoyed helping develop Joe and his team. He wanted to do more of this with other companies. Bob was able to get very clear on his Why and had a compelling story to share, yet he still struggled to figure out how to convince other business owners to work with him.

Like Ethan, Bob is struggling with how to explain what he has done for the past couple of decades. Knowing your Why is a good start. How we translate it and communicate it is where the magic happens.

I'll provide a framework for creating a plan, a brand, messaging, and a go-to-market strategy for the expertise you have spent decades developing, the problems you solve, and aligning that with companies that value it.

CHAPTER 6

Create Your Executive Brand

Without a brand, you are likely seen as the typical "consultant who decided to hang a shingle out and see what happened." The importance of building an executive brand has been on the rise in the past 15–20 years. There are few executives, such as my father, who spent his entire first career with one company. Executives are moving companies, locations, and careers at an increasing rate. Regardless of the move or change, the goal is to represent your brand instead of a company brand and have that brand move with you. Ideally, it helps guide your direction and eases your transition to the next thing.

It is important to create the right brand to convey the impact you can create for your clients. One of the biggest challenges for executives with long careers is in communicating what they can do for potential clients. Those wanting to market themselves independently have to create a brand to get the right message across. Not everyone with whom an executive comes in contact can spend hours discussing backgrounds, resumés, CVs, and bios to understand what they have done, what they do best, and how they can help companies. Instead, they must rely on small snippets of information and messaging to convey the key points.

An executive brand is what people say about you when you are not in the room. It is, ideally, defined by you. Creating an executive brand takes time and effort, but it can become one of the most useful and effective tools in building your business.

When I first met Ethan, he was determined to build a sustainable pipeline. He had been working diligently for months on his marketing. He hired someone to help him build a website and assist with his messaging, and he was working with a few other executives on business referrals. Ethan was giving an overview of what he did and how he helped companies. He was very excited about the headline on his home page, "Business Transformation." He then went on to talk about all the various ways he transforms businesses through process re-engineering, culture change, etc. About 50 minutes into the phone call, he shared a story about how he led an acquisition of a company that was on the verge of bankruptcy. The CEO had asked Ethan to lead the division that was created to absorb the acquired company. Two years after the initial acquisition, Ethan had grown it more than 800%. It was in the black with $220 million in profit. My response was, "Why are you waiting until this point in the conversation to mention this?" I believe that is called burying the lead. It should be the headline.

Your brand is your newspaper headline. If an article is being done about you, what will the headline say? This is the first slide (or page) of your business plan. Another way to think of it is as your "Call me when" statement. This has become popular in networking circles. For example, I say, "Call me when a company is struggling with its leadership team — there isn't one, there's lots of turnover, or the company has outgrown the team's skills."

I asked Ethan if he wants to be called every time a company is on the verge of bankruptcy. Before I could finish the sentence, Ethan responded, "No." Ethan was clear on his Why: He enjoys helping companies be better versions of themselves. He was also clear about not wanting to lead turnarounds for the next 10 years. He struggled with what he did want to lean into, what he enjoys doing, and how to communicate it.

What is Your Expertise?

The most common myth I hear is that if you focus on just one area, you may miss an opportunity or an engagement, because you can help clients in a variety of areas. The reality is that you are more likely to be missing out on more opportunities because your peers don't know when and how to recommend you. This is caused by casting too wide a net. If there's an opportunity to refer someone, people are more likely to refer someone who is a specialist in the company's need and situation, rather than someone who says, "I help companies grow."

As a seasoned executive, Ethan has a diverse skill set. He has worked in and managed many business areas, but he was cautious about calling himself an expert in any particular area. I appreciated his hesitation. Though he has been responsible for and led human resources, operations, and legal, he isn't an expert in any of these areas.

So how does Ethan figure out what he is an expert at?

He can start by asking himself the question, "Right now, if I had to get up on stage in front of 50 of my peers, what subject or situation could I speak about as an expert?" This includes being able to cite multiple case studies or examples. To make his point and relate it to real situations, he would relate a story about what had been happening, what he did to intervene, and why it was so successful.

If you can't stand up in front of your peers, with confidence, and teach them something they either don't know or are being offered a new perspective on, be cautious of presenting yourself as an expert on the topic. Another way of looking at it: If you were to ask 10 former supervisors, peers, or clients to rate you on a scale from one to five, with five being the highest, would they rate you a four or five in the area?

I see the term expert used broadly at the executive level, especially when an executive has grown a company and been part of establishing the marketing, sales, accounting, finance, and operations. Narrow your focus down to what situations you can be dropped into and be the expert.

I advised Ethan to start by identifying what he does best and what he enjoys most — both at the same time. This point of intersection is where he is unstoppable.

If you're the go-to person for specific types of situations, people will want to know that, because this is where you are more likely to succeed and perform best. Compare that with "what a company is willing to pay for and what they see value in," and you are headed in the right direction.

I had Ethan walk through this exercise to find the patterns or trends in his background:

- List at least 10 accomplishments you have been proud of in your past and, more importantly, ones for which you thoroughly enjoyed the process. This list isn't for your resumé, but rather for your introspection, so stay honest, and don't think it through too much.

- Think about your accomplishments, and note what steps you took to achieve them. Itemize all the steps under each one of your accomplishments, and you'll likely notice a common denominator.

Ethan thought about this. He struggled at first, so he did take a look at all the accomplishments on his resumé. He started noticing a physical reaction to those he remembered fondly and others that made him tense up as he read them. He enjoyed talking to customers and learning about how they used a product, and what they liked and didn't like about it. He liked talking to the marketing and sales teams and helping them connect the dots between what the customers were saying and what they were doing. It was like a light bulb going on in their heads. The more he wrote, the more he smiled and continued his list.

What Value do you Offer? Do you Solve the Problem?

We can have the greatest product, service, or delivery mechanism anyone has ever heard of, but if a client doesn't value it or understand the value it can provide, we end up like Ethan, with a lot to offer but no one willing to sign up for it.

This can range from how you solve the problem to something unique in your background. For example, do you have an exit-planning certification or PMP, do you have a proven process you customize for each client (this is seen as evidence that you are an expert), or have you done something 15 times (15 exits, 15 plant relocations, etc.)?

What is the value from the company's perspective? The WIIFM: What's In It For Me? If your solution set includes utilizing external employee evaluation tools, such as profiling tools, and the company CEO does not believe in personality assessments, is this a company you want to work with? Are those tools the same? No. Do you want to spend your time explaining that to the CEO and convincing them about the value of it? Likely not. They may have a problem you can solve, but they don't value how you solve it.

When you approach things from the perspective of the client and the problems they are having or the outcome they want to get to, it is easier to connect with the right opportunities. For example: "I help small to mid-size companies ensure they have accurate and timely financials on a monthly basis." Or, "I help business owners transition from being VP of sales to being CEO." Note: I am leading with the problem I solve, not necessarily that I do it as a fractional CFO or fractional VP of sales. Stating our service without stating the pain we solve in the market is like saying, "I sell knives." Are these for hunting, fishing, cooking (everyday cooking or high end), etc.? What is the application of the product or service, or what problem are they solving? "I help home cooks act like professional chefs with no fear of cutting themselves." If you know what I am like in the kitchen, you know why I am sold at this statement alone. I don't care about size, color, name, cost. No more keeping Band-Aids in the kitchen!

As Ethan looked through the list and compared it with the list where he was most impactful in his career and enjoyed it the most, he started to see the picture coming together. He knew he was good at helping businesses figure out how to grow and make money. Where he started to see the connections was in how he was able to repeatedly grow businesses or parts of businesses in the most profitable way possible. Once he understood how he was able to do it and his secret sauce, the pieces of his brand started to fall into place.

I suggested that Ethan call three people who have worked with him before to ask them what value he brought to their situation. To Ethan's delight, their comments aligned with the picture that was forming in his head. The golden nugget was how they explained it. He wrote down what they said word-for-word. They used terms such as simplicity and clarity. He noticed they described pain points they were having and said he helped them quickly get to the answer. Ethan was so excited. He started to see why he hadn't gotten much traction the past six months. No one had understood what he did, the problems he solved, or the value he could bring!

This exercise can be especially helpful for executives who have a mix of backgrounds, such as operations and technology. In conversations with referral partners and potential clients, you may be talking about how you provide operational efficiencies and improved processes through technology. In your mind, this is the value you bring your clients. However, if you talk to one of your clients, the conversation would be more centered around how you stepped into an enterprise resource planning (ERP) implementation process that was going off-track. In their minds, you helped join the operations of the business with the technology that was there to support its needs, rather than letting the technology dictate how the company should function. Make the shift to describing what you do in terms of the problems clients are experiencing rather than what it is you actually do.

It is helpful to step back and stop thinking like an executive or a consultant. Think more like a client. Put yourself in their shoes.

Potential Clients: Who has These Problems? To Whom are you Selling?

The more focused you are, the easier it is for you to identify your target market, for people to remember what you do, and for them to be able to think of you when they hear the issue you are best at solving.

By understanding what type of work we want to do and what problems we solve, we can start to profile what types of companies have this need. As much clarity as Ethan was starting to get, he still thought every company needed his help. As great as the concept is to have your potential market be every company that is in business, it is most marketers' biggest nightmare. But how could he possibly narrow it down?

One of the most helpful tools in figuring this out is by listening to others as they try to figure out a similar situation. We are able to take ourselves out of our situation and watch someone else's movie. The plot and the storyline are much easier to see. We can then apply that to our situation and gain some much-needed clarity. I invited Ethan to join an independent executive roundtable I host.

One of the executives at the roundtable that day, Larry, was an executive whose history centered around product marketing. He wanted to transition to interim work and have more flexibility around whom he worked with and what types of situations he helped. He simply was not ready to go back to a direct-hire situation. He introduced himself as an interim vice president of product marketing. He asked how many interim vice president of product marketing roles I see. As we discussed what size company would have a role such as this on a part-time or interim full-time basis, it greatly reduced the companies with which he could work. While this does give him a small target market, it did not align with his Why. He had worked with large companies his entire career. He wants to be more hands-on and wants to work with a growing business, not a mature one. We started brainstorming what problems he solves rather than the type of work he has done. Once we were done, he identified a couple of common problems he could apply more broadly to the types of companies he wants to work with. He helps companies figure out why their product isn't selling and create a roadmap to maximize its market potential. He is solving the problem of "why this isn't working" followed by the next problem of "how do we get it working." He thought through the types of products, companies, and industries he had worked in. With the help of the group, he was able to narrow it down to a few related industries and problems he solved in them.

I could see Ethan still wanted to knock on every business' proverbial door, and explain what he does, since he now had some clarity on how to explain it.

We went around the table and had each person identify a segment they would focus on for the next 90 days. This didn't mean they wouldn't accept an introduction or work with a company outside this segment. It is a tool to narrow focus and create a straighter line to get to the clients we want to work with faster.

This segment could be by products, industries, types of companies, sizes of companies, types of transitions, and so on. I challenged the group to make the connection between the problems they solve and who or what type of company or situation most likely had those problems.

- If you are a human resources expert, and your skill set is engaging employees who are not in the same place, then you are looking for companies with multiple sites or a virtual employee base.
- If you have spent the past 10 years in companies with partnerships or family-owned businesses, this is a great way to segment. One of the busiest CPAs I have ever known introduced herself as a specialist for partnerships in the construction industry.
- If you want to make an impact and help determine the direction a company is going, then you are most likely working with founder-led companies.

As you get clarity on who has the problems you solve, it should be integrated into your messaging:

- I help software companies develop the go-to-market strategy when launching a new product.
- I help second-generation, family-owned businesses transition to the next generation's vision.
- I help small, privately owned companies build a profitable infrastructure, so the owner can take more time off and have money to invest in growth opportunities.

I wrapped up the session with one of my favorite exercises:

Imagine you are meeting someone for the first time at an event, and they ask you, "What do you do?" The answer to this question should be one short phrase that effectively communicates your work.

It can take this form:

"I help [your target market] facing [the situation they are typically in, a.k.a., "their problem"] to get results, such as [an example of what you have done for a client]."

Fill in the blanks, and you'll have a one-sentence answer that helps the listener understand and remember what you do. As you refine it, you can adjust the verbiage, add a story, and have a compelling introduction that is impactful and memorable.

The week after the roundtable, Larry called to tell me about a virtual networking event he attended. He ended up in a breakout group of four. He was excited to test out his new statement. It was his turn, and it slid out like he'd been saying it for years: "I help SaaS technology companies improve their go-to-market when they are struggling with lead generation and close rates."

The business coach on the call raised her hand and said, "I have a client I need to introduce you to." What if he had said, "I am an interim VP of product marketing, and I work with companies in healthcare, manufacturing, technology, and medical devices"? The business coach likely would not have been able to easily make the connection between her

SaaS client who is struggling with lead generation and how Larry could help. Larry led with the pain he solves and what type of company most likely has this problem. This aligns with his Why and his experience; it is his secret sauce.

I was wondering how Ethan felt after the session and reached out to see what he had come up with. He admitted his head was still spinning, and he was struggling with how to take his 30-year career and put it into a sentence. We discussed some of the feedback he got from the calls he made. He thought about something a former employer said. He realized the discussion and exercises we were going through were similar to what has helped him be so successful at growing businesses.

He said:

"I help founder/CEOs with stalled or slow growth, get clarity on where they want to go, determine who they need on their team, and create a roadmap on how to get there. I have done this multiple times in my career, including turning around a bankrupt company into 800x growth and profitability in two years."

All I could do was smile. Ethan had figured out what problem he wanted to solve, whom he wanted to help, and the impact he wanted to make. He had gotten to know me well enough to know his journey was far from over. In my mind, he had just gotten started. Ethan would now get to explore all the possibilities for the role he can have in helping founder-led organizations jumpstart their growth.

CHAPTER 7

Business Model: What's Your Role in the Solution?

Independent executives have struggled for years trying to figure out whether to brand themselves as an interim executive, consultant, advisor, fractional executive, etc. There are many options for a business to solve their challenges. There are as many options for how an independent executive can support those challenges as a standalone solution or part of a solution set. Deciding whether you want to do that on an interim or fractional basis is dependent on how you want to work with the company and structure the contract. Here are some of the more common options for how an independent executive can step in and help a company:

- Interim
- Fractional
- Project-based
- Board Director/Advisor
- Coach

When I first started writing about the various terms, my hypothesis was that they were all essentially the same thing. The difference was whatever term the user had been introduced to first. If you heard a fellow CEO talk about their interim CFO, then you used the term interim.

I see the various terms growing in popularity when referring to the work arrangement and how it is being structured. Some may use it as part of their branding or differentiation. In reality, it helps the independent executive better define how they want to structure their business. Here are some examples:

Interim/Temporary Executive

The terms *interim* and *temporary* can be used interchangeably. *Interim* currently is the more popular of the two and has a big head start with its wide acceptance in various parts of the world. From an executive's perspective, this refers to accepting assignments that are not intended to be ongoing. It could be part-time or full-time interim.

What this option looks like for you: The executive has flexibility to take on a role that is 3–5 days a week. They enjoy solving pressing issues, stabilizing the situation, and putting future growth plans in place. Once the heavy lifting is done, they enjoy transitioning it to the internal team or a new team member and moving on to the next assignment. Most enjoy having one company to focus on at a time.

Fractional/Part Time

Fractional has overtaken the term part time when referring to companies using only part of an executive's schedule. This is used when an executive wants to work with multiple companies, typically 1–2 days a week with each one. The need and the contract are ongoing; the role is likely needed until the company grows to the point of justifying a full-time, direct-hire cost, and it is clear and consistent about what they need longer term. This can be applied to just about any role in the company and is most commonly used for fractional CFOs. Why? On a company's growth curve, the finance executive is the first leadership position needed beyond the founder(s). The need starts early. Most companies don't need a full-time CFO until later in its growth curve.

What this option looks like for you: This is ongoing with multiple clients. The executive enjoys consistency and is good with variety. There may be personal reasons the executive only wants to fill three or four days a week of time, which means they would be limited to interim work if they can't take anything five days a week. I have talked to many executives who can't imagine helping a company and making an impact in as little as 1–2 days a week, and they don't like working with more than one company at a time. Others make an incredible career out of this type of work. We are not all built the same way.

Project-Based

An executive is brought in to complete a specific task or deliverable. It is typically completed within a short time frame and has a clear beginning and end/deliverable. This is a great option when your skill set or the scope is easily defined, controlled, and/or repetitive. We see this approach most commonly in the following situations:

- An executive decides they want to leave a company to be independent or to have more flexibility in their schedule. The company may need some continued support from the executive for specific projects. Due to their familiarity with the company, what is needed, and the deliverables, the executive may continue to work for the company on a project basis.
- Assessments: These tend to be predictable, finite in time, and a valuable deliverable for the company. They are a low-risk option for both the executive and the company.
- Productization: We'll discuss this more later in the book. Any time an executive can segment their expertise to a single solution set with specific deliverables and a consistent statement of work, it is a win–win for both the executive and the company.

What this option looks like for you: If you are doing large-scale consulting projects, this tends to be a long sales process, involving some kind of RFP or proposal and, likely, multiple resources. On the other end, this is one of the most valuable tools for go-to-market with small to mid-size businesses. Given the range of services this can cover, this may look different for each independent executive. It is highly customizable and complementary.

Board Director/Advisor

The executive's expertise is of great value to the company and is available as needed to provide insights and advice. This can be done ad hoc or at regularly scheduled meetings. This is typically done on a monthly retainer and covers as little as a few hours a month up to a couple of days a month. Once the company needs more than that, from an executive's perspective, it tends to go into fractional or interim. The executive steps into the business and puts pencil to paper. They are producing rather than advising. Some executives will take the business, while others are clear it is not their model and refer it out. We'll get into this in more detail later.

What this option looks like for you: This gives an executive a lot of variety at a 50,000-foot level. An executive enjoys helping by asking the right questions, providing feedback, and making sure the owner or CEO has the company going in the right direction. The executive could be working with five or more clients at a time. The executive has a proven track record of success and enjoys helping others achieve the same success.

Coach

Since the nature of the work is well defined and does not include being hands-on in the organization, think of this as an advisory role. There are a number of certifications and trainings for business and executive coaching, which lend more structure to the industry than most of the categories above. The coaching industry has also evolved. The distinctions and productization of the following are well developed:

- **Business coaching**: focuses on the business and its goals. This may involve working with the owner, the CEO, or a combination of individuals. The outcomes and deliverables are company-centric.
- **CEO coaching**: focuses on the CEO and the CEO's goals, which can be a combination of professional and personal. The outcomes and deliverables are person-centric.
- **Leadership team coaching**: working with them as individuals and/or as a team. The outcomes and deliverables are focused on alignment, goal achievement, and development for each stage of the company.
- **Leadership development**: This can be for individuals who are currently in leadership roles or are emerging leaders. This is a great option for executives who enjoy mentoring and training. This can be industry specific or functionally specific. For example, developing technicians who have been identified as future leaders or recent college graduates within an industry.

What this option looks like for you: This can be done on a one-to-one basis or as a group. This approach can be easily productized, sold as a webinar, or even offered with many options to multiply revenue opportunities. It is a great choice for someone who is a people person. They love helping people grow and develop skills. You can be working for 15 or more clients at a single time. They could all be at different companies or within the same company.

Direct Hire

This can be the executive's primary goal or be an outcome of any of the above. This is traditionally seen as an "all or nothing" option, but it doesn't have to be. We'll discuss this more later in the book. This is not always a binary decision and can be combined with independent executive activities that benefit both the executive and the company.

What this option looks like for you: The executive enjoys having the stability, does not want to always be doing business development, likes being part of an ongoing leadership team, and has flexibility in their life to dedicate much of their time to what the company needs vs. other commitments.

Deciding What Works for You

Looking at it from the perspective of the individual bringing the solution, you get to determine how you want to work with companies and what your solution looks like.

Here is an example using a company's problem and the various perspectives an independent executive may have on whether they are the right fit and want to say "yes" or "no" to it.

Situation: I have a client who needs someone to clean up their chart of accounts, convert them from cash to accrual, set up monthly financial reporting they can trust and get on time, then rinse and repeat every month. This means an executive will need to have some ongoing time available at the beginning of the month, likely a few hours a week as things come up, and some additional availability the first three months to get everything set up. I asked a couple of executives if they are interested. Here are their responses:

- **Executive 1**: "No, thank you. I am just finishing up an interim assignment that will wind down next month. I have a 4-week vacation planned and will be ready for another interim assignment when I get back. Do you have anything 4–5 days a week — preferably another exit — starting in two months?"
- **Executive 2**: "No, thank you. I am only doing advisory work at this point. I just had a big financial exit with a client I was an interim for and then stepped in as their COO to get them sold. It was intense. I can help advise or be on a board if the company is looking to exit, but I am not looking to do much more than that right now."
- **Executive 3**: "That may work. I have a client I am winding down — they hired someone full time — and I have room for one to two new clients at this point. I can hold off on taking any other new clients until I get this client all set up. I don't mind working a few weekends the first month or two. Yes, I can make that work."

When discussing with Ethan what works best for him, we used a different perspective and reviewed the following situations:

Your role	How you are helping
Owner's Box	Asking the right questions and guiding
	Not inside the business
	Advisor, Board
Coach	More strategic and planning
	Engagement is structured
	Consultant, Project-Based
Quarterback	Inside doing the work, owning initiatives, leading the way
	Can be strategic or tactical
	Interim, Fractional, Direct Hire
Supporting Player	Filling gaps, often as an SME
	Interim, Fractional, Direct Hire

As we talked through each of these, Ethan did not have any personal situations that would affect whether he had to limit his schedule or his travel. He knew he wasn't going to be able to help the founder and the leadership team get clarity on what they were doing and create a plan for them as a coach or advisor. He could see himself as an advisor eventually, but there was going to be a lot of work up front before he got to that point. He wasn't sure he wanted to step in and take on an active role. He liked the idea of being an added resource, allowing him to own the solution and the roadmap, and support execution through influence, not direct management.

He saw himself as a coach versus being in the owner's box or a coach. As he got this clarity, he could start to see the types of situations in which he could be effective and those he would likely pass on. Fortunately for Ethan, he was creating a business, not just a pipeline, that would give him the platform to pick what he wanted to do and didn't want to do while never saying, "I can't help you with that."

Like Ethan, we now know what our product/service is, what problems we are solving, who has these problems, and how to differentiate ourselves, and we have an effective way to communicate it through our executive brand. Now the fun part: how to make sure we aren't a best-kept secret.

CHAPTER 8

Communicating Your Brand/USP

One thing remains true: The more focused the brand and messaging about an executive's expertise, how they help companies, and whom they help, the more likely the executive is to be remembered and referred.

I get to meet and work with incredible executives who have remarkable careers. Their resumés include CEO or executive leadership roles with known brands, or they helped sell a brand no one has ever heard of for $100 million. Whether I am spending two minutes with them or two hours, every accomplishment they have ever had doesn't matter if I either can't understand a word they say, or it goes in one ear and out the other. While I can take full responsibility for not having enough of a knowledge base for their industry or for having an attention span like that of a typical business owner (25 words or less), the reality is that I am the typical audience for most executives looking for their next job, contract or otherwise. To be able to understand it, relate to it, and remember it, I need a brand to be clear, consistent, and memorable.

Clear

I think every company I work with needs some form of change management and transformation. However, these are two terms I have never used on a call with a client, unless they brought it up first and specifically requested it.

This is how the conversation would go if I did use these terms:

- **Me**: "We help companies transform and scale through change management and culture alignment."
- **Person on the other end**: "So, you're calling my baby ugly. I don't need my company transformed, I don't need any big changes, and our culture is fine. I just need to double my sales in the next two years, stop losing money, and stop losing so many good employees."

When communicating what you do and how you help, be aware of the words being used. The more we speak to the pain points, the easier it is for both parties to understand each other. Something as simple as "accountability" can cause a disconnect. I am a business owner, working 12-hour days, buried in running the company as the CEO, CFO, and VP of sales. I see things not getting done in a timely manner, and I have to task my team for anything to get done. I don't see a lack of accountability (regardless of who is causing it). What is simple and easy to see from the outside looking in is not as simple and easy when you are inside looking around.

Ethan's simplified version of, "I give businesses a roadmap for how they can grow" is a lot easier to understand than, "I do business transformation."

Exercise: Your Recipe

One exercise that can help is to write out all the steps you go through to deliver an outcome to a company (as an interim, fractional, advisor, direct hire). Think of this as your recipe. This exercise will also help later when we discuss productization. Listing out what you go through to get to "business transformation" can help simplify it into recognizable and understandable steps for a potential client. We can start to see how it applies to our company and our situation. It is also easier to see the outcome we want when we better understand what gets done to get there.

We can take this a step further and check the competitive landscape for what we are offering. What type of information comes up in a search engine when you type in "business transformation," "helping a company scale," or "[insert how you describe what you do here]"? Do the top two consulting firms have white papers explaining what it is, or is there a variety of articles on the five steps to accomplishing it? The first has us competing in a highly saturated, hard-to-understand landscape; that's why large firms are writing white papers on it. The latter is easier to brand, communicate, and have common language on. When it can be broken down into five steps, we open our options for narrowing our initial offering or our entry point even more to the first couple of steps. We can turn the steps into an infographic. We'll touch on each of these more when we discuss productization and thought leadership.

Ethan found this useful to further refine his messaging. He was able to articulate how he figured out what a company should be focusing on to achieve the company's No. 1 goal: how to get alignment among the company leadership, and with their help, create the roadmap (a.k.a., a plan) for what needed to get done. He was able to make his secret sauce into a recipe.

Market Testing for Clarity

Two people can be talking about the same thing but describing it in two different ways. Each person has their own perspective and will apply what you do to that perspective and their experiences. If you are basing the messaging of your brand solely on what you come up with on your own, you may be off the mark, given the importance of your referral network and your potential client's perspective. You want to describe what you can do for companies in the same or similar words your potential clients would use to describe it. The best source to figure this out is past clients or colleagues with whom you have worked. The words you use and the point you are getting across should be phrased from their perspective. Be careful of focusing too much on what you want, and keep in mind what your potential clients need.

As a double check, call five people, and share your brand: your service, what problems you solve, for whom you solve them, and the value you bring. Are they able to easily understand it, explain it back to you, and ask follow-up questions about it? Once we have an easily understandable brand, we have our clarity.

Consistent

I met an executive who was looking to do interim CEO work. I reviewed his resumé and saw a series of COO and CFO roles. I looked up his LinkedIn profile, and the only roles that were in view were board roles. The lack of consistency between the work he wanted to do and what was being communicated only caused me confusion.

As an independent executive, it is now all about you and your brand. Manage your brand the same way a Fortune 500 company would manage theirs. Is your information and the look and feel across your online and offline footprints consistent? If two people meet and find out they both know you, would they both say essentially the same thing about you? What is that? What they say should be consistent with the brand you want. Executives have a range of opportunities to convey their brand. I will address a few of the most common ones and provide guidance on common stumbling blocks.

The Resumé Conundrum

How we present our decades of history on paper is the resumé conundrum.

Using a resumé is a widely accepted form of establishing credibility through the companies you have worked for, the roles you have had, and what you have accomplished.

You can talk to 10 different people, including clients and search firms, and get a different answer about what your resumé should look like, what should be on it, etc. The reason for that is resumés, like any good marketing materials, are situation specific. However, the more you narrow the type of work and your messaging, the fewer situations you will need to account for.

It is always easier to use a third-party example rather than ourselves. Think through the marketing materials for a healthy food brand. The more options available and geographies being targeted, the more the marketing collateral needs to be customized. Well-known and established brands have expanded options — a marketing campaign for each market and one that shifts monthly or quarterly including new product introductions. The key phrase is "known and established." They have grown into it, and they have the budget for it. They likely started with a narrow offering in one marketplace and proved it out before expanding. This is a good starting point as you are establishing your brand. It will also help keep it consistent across platforms and narrow the need for multiple resumés, bios, decks, etc.

Guidelines for direct-hire work will vary from this, since so many executive roles are based on job descriptions that include the kitchen sink, the junk draw, and "all other duties as assigned." Generally speaking, if you are clear on your brand and the types of direct-hire roles you want, the tweaks and customizations will be significantly reduced.

I look at everything online as part of an executive's resumé, since we never know what someone will look at first: our website (if we have one), our actual resumé, our LinkedIn profile, an article we wrote, etc. To avoid confusion, I'll refer to it as an online footprint. Think of your online footprint as being consistent with what you would put at the top of the home page of your website. Everything out there should have the same brand, have similar visual and verbal messaging, and be a collection of supportive marketing materials for your brand.

What your online footprint looks like will depend on the type of work you want. There are various options for presenting your expertise, establishing credibility, and showing relevance (the translation element) to the problems you solve.

For example:

- **Advisor or board profile**: Give a background overview establishing your high-level experience, build trust and establish credibility with testimonials, show relevance and accomplishments with case studies.
- **Presentation style profile**: Great if you have a process, tools, or a different way to display prior results or accomplishments. If you are a marketer, this could include a slide with the brands you have worked on; for operations, it could be a five-step process you use to go from evaluation to execution.
- **Chronological profile**: This is the more traditional layout, listing each company and role chronologically, starting with the most recent.
- **Functional profile**: This entails pulling the key accomplishments out of a chronological resumé and summarizing them by categories or roles: human capital, fundraising, M&A. Work experience (company, role) can then be listed after, with one company and role per line. Dates become less important on a functional resumé, so it is situational if you want to keep them in or leave them out.

It all comes down to "it depends." What does your background/work history look like: Have you been in full-time roles, or do you have 10 years of being an interim? What is the purpose of it: direct hire, interim work, fractional work, or board work? Who is receiving it: a system that needs to read, import, and segment into fields; a referral partner who will pass it along; the head of HR; or a potential client you just met?

Whichever you choose, it should be consistent across the various platforms and communications, including profiles, information you send via email, a website (if you chose to have one), online posts, articles, podcasts, videos, etc.

I receive a lot of questions around listing experience for contract work. This can be done under the title of "Independent Roles" or your independent executive company name. If you are listing five different interim roles, "Interim Roles" makes sense. If you are just starting and will be listing your brand information along with a brief description of a pro bono project you did recently (whether you disclose it was pro bono is up to you), listing it under your company name makes sense. If you do list your company name, be cautious in using CEO or president-type titles for your independent business. When talking through resumés with clients, more times than not, they see the title of the independent executive's business and comment: "I see they are currently a CEO and working for a company. Why do they want to leave a role like that?" It takes some detailed reading and additional thought or explanation for some to connect the dots. Make it clear and easy for the reader, whether it is on a resumé or an online profile.

Memorable

Just telling people your accomplishments may not be enough. Package your brand into a *memorable* example that explains to the referral partner how you work and can help clients, or to potential clients how you can affect their business.

No matter how many people we meet or connect with, they first need to remember what we do in order to refer us. There is nothing more frustrating (for me), than to connect with someone I haven't talked to in a while and have them say: "Shoot! I needed an interim executive a couple of months ago, and I completely forgot about you." Despite how memorable I may be, what I do and how I help companies also needs to be memorable.

Ask yourself, "What do I want to be remembered for?" As we have previously discussed, contrary to most instincts, the more you niche your expertise, the more you will get referred. Why? A specialized skill set is easier to remember and makes it easier for others to recognize opportunities for you.

If I meet you, and I hear, "I help CEOs bridge the gap between where they are and where they want their company to be," to whom would I refer you? There is too much brain work needed to figure out when to refer you in, so I am unlikely to remember you, what you do, or how you can help.

Another common statement I hear is, "I help drive revenues through innovation." Increasing revenues through innovation has become a buzz phrase and broad topic; it is not as helpful when trying to understand what your expertise is and what you can do for a company. Why work with you instead of the three other revenue-driving interim executives who have been introduced to me recently?

Let's say you are passionate about productivity. You have done well as an operations executive. When listing your accomplishments and how you achieved them, your "smile moment" was listing out all the ways you have helped people get more time into their days through simplicity and efficiency, leaving them more minutes or hours to spend with their family or on their passion projects. To make yourself memorable, you can say your passion for productivity helps people find more time in their day to do what they are passionate about. You can add a numerical component to help illustrate how much time can be saved or how much money they can add to the profit of their company. There is a reason Geico still uses the line, "Fifteen minutes could save you 15% or more on car insurance." Numbers are impactful and easy to remember.

Your online footprint can tie into productivity scenarios and stories. You can share your daily activities in posts about what you did to be more productive. Every time someone sees your name, it is accompanied by an article, post, comment, or meme about how a company or individual can become more productive; the brand is continually reinforced. The moment someone in your network hears a CEO talking about productivity or related topics, such as feeling overworked or getting too many emails and not being able to manage them all, they immediately think of you. Because you have also tied it to passion projects, those who have met you use you as an example any time someone talks about wanting more time to do what they love. You are emulating what they want to do. They may not think of you if the company is having an issue with inventory, which you certainly can help with based on your prior roles, but you'd much prefer referral partners to remember you 10 times for productivity than once for three other problems.

You can also integrate the two popular techniques to help people remember you:

- Numbers
- Stories

The Power of Numbers

You are no longer VP of sales or COO for XYZ Corp. You are a problem-solver. You no longer have a list of your roles and responsibilities; you have a list of ways you have helped clients. In your conversations, be clear on "here's the type of issues I solve." Most companies don't say: "I'm looking for a part-time VP of sales" or "I need someone with sales management expertise." Instead, they say, "I have a sales problem," but they leave out that they are looking for someone to solve it. To help with that, make yourself impressive and memorable. Nothing does that better than numbers. You want someone to be able to meet you today and remember the types of problems you have solved and what kind of impact you have made weeks or months later.

The more easily referral sources can remember this information, the more they will remember you when the next CEO is discussing their sales issues. They will remember your story about a similar sales situation and the results you got for the client.

I have reviewed thousands of resumés and profiles. Quantifying an executive's accomplishments is the biggest gap and the first request from clients. "What have they accomplished in the past, and what types of results have they delivered for other companies?" Given the tremendous amount of experience an executive has, clients looking to bring on an interim executive or advisor are not looking for whether they had profit and loss (PNL) responsibility. That is assumed at this point. What impact the executive has had on PNL is what they are more concerned about. Leave the job responsibilities on the CV, and focus on the results you have accomplished in your past couple of positions or projects.

Don't be modest, and don't be stingy with numbers. As much as clients do appreciate that you "increased morale," they are far more impressed that you "reduced turnover by 20%." By how much did you help grow sales or improve EBITDA? A client is looking for specific results.

- Rather than, "I increased sales," say, "Sales increased by 32% year-over-year, while the operating budget was reduced by 5%."
- Rather than, "I am a versatile executive with more than 20 years of experience in the C-suite who can help companies maximize value and increase returns," consider using a specific example that exemplifies what you can do for a company: "I have more than 20 years of experience working with startup companies in the energy industry. The past three firms I worked with each exited within five years for multiples of 8 to 10 times EBIDTA."

Another common description is, "I work with small, growing companies and help them get past the curve where their sales have outgrown the talent of their team." Try adding at least one specific example, such as, "I helped the last company I worked with grow from $10 million to a run rate of $18 million and increase their net profit by 50% in the nine months I was there."

Don't Say it, Story It.

Never underestimate the value of a good story. I have used this strategy throughout this book. It is easier to remember someone and what they are great at when you can tie it to a story. We use stories to teach new concepts to children. Stories are used in various cultures to pass on teachings. They help bring concepts to life, especially mundane or difficult-to-understand concepts. You can even use part of your story when introducing yourself in a group setting. The audience will need to connect with you further to get more of the story, especially if you leave out the punchline.

Great keynote speakers have mastered the art of storytelling to convey concepts to large audiences. How do you get a group of 300+ people to walk away with the same message? Through stories. Go back to the list of accomplishments you created to narrow down your expertise. I have no doubt there are a couple of good stories in there to convey the impact you can bring to companies.

Fortunately, you don't need an audience of 300+ to know if your brand messaging is hitting the mark. As with any good marketing campaign, market testing and audience reaction can be invaluable. For an independent executive, a personal advisory board can be the same. At the beginning of this section, I mentioned calling up five people and testing out your brand. Establishing a personal advisory board can serve this purpose, as well. Here are some options for this:

- **Outreach**: Contact people who know you well and you trust to be good sounding boards to give you honest feedback. You can include a few people you recently met.
- **Live scenario**: Use any introduction or networking situation to test out your brand and messaging. See what questions you get. Ask your own clarifying questions to see if it was clear.
- **Formalize it**: Get a group together monthly, bimonthly, or quarterly for a meal. Make it an affinity group (golfing, other independent

executives, leaders you have worked with, etc.). Create your own peer group. They will appreciate it as much as you do.

I discussed one of the challenges of being independent as being a business of one. Building an advisory board, or situations and networks that serve as an advisory board, can help mitigate this. It can also help you leverage one of my favorite topics, thought leadership.

Thought Leadership

Being a thought leader is the most powerful way to share your brand and have it be clear, consistent, and memorable.

A great way to establish yourself as the expert and create value for potential prospects is to publish consumable and engaging content. You likely won't be meeting all your future clients at networking events; they will come from other sources, such as referral partners or your online presence. Information about what you do and how you address pains in the marketplace that can be easily consumed by your target audience is worthy of time and investment. Content can be in the form of articles/blogs, posts (including commenting on someone else's post), slide decks, presentations, speaking opportunities, podcasts, webinars, videos, online trainings/classes, etc.

Even if you don't see yourself as a writer, there are too many options available for this to be your stumbling block. Be careful of falling into the same trap when it comes to creating content as clients do when they don't address the issues they have: The "do nothing" option. It is human nature to shy away from what doesn't come naturally to us. It is worth making ourselves uncomfortable for a period of time to try out different formats and figure out what does feel natural (or at least not painful).

My husband and I are not naturally social individuals, so it was no surprise that our son didn't automatically walk up to people and introduce himself. It took years to have him walk up to someone and say, "Thank you," or knock on someone's door to sell popcorn or ask for his ball back when it was kicked over the fence. It was days of agony for him to get up the courage to ask a neighbor, with whom he'd had past interactions, for his ball back. He came home recently from spending a few weeks with his grandparents and recounted the number of times his ball went into the bushes, into the street, hit the sliding glass door, and one time, into the neighbor's yard. My husband and I had an over/under on how long it took him to get the ball back from the neighbor. When he took a breath, we asked what happened when the ball went into the neighbor's yard. Without even pausing, he told us that, as soon as it happened, he went over, rang the doorbell, and got it back. He could clearly see the shock on our faces. His response: "What did I have to lose? I had more to gain by getting my ball back." We often have more to gain by trying something that doesn't come naturally to us. Give it a try, and see what happens.

There is rarely an interaction you have or something you accomplish that can't be turned into content. Look for ways to leverage your expertise or your engagements. Here are a few examples to help you brainstorm some ways to make it work for you:

- A simple online post showcasing your expertise. For example, "Great client meeting today — young CEO with great insights needs me to help determine next growth strategy for his company." No need to disclose any details or the company/CEO name. If the CEO is OK with it, include a picture of the two of you (again, no need, if they prefer to not be mentioned). It could also be a fun meme about the concept you are addressing. Add in an extra couple of lines giving your advice for companies considering a growth strategy next year.

- Record yourself recapping a recent assignment, a major accomplishment and how you did it, or a recent conversation you were passionate about. Anyone with video-call access can record and use a transcription app. Many now include a summary for you, making it all too easy.

- Similar to the previous idea, but make it a two-way conversation. Interview someone, or have someone interview you. Align it with your brand. It can be done in some very creative ways; ask your advisory board. This can be transcribed for a written post or article, as well as a video or podcast.

- If you are not a technologist and not good with apps, hire someone to ghostwrite, transcribe, or clean up the video.

- Create a briefing or case study of a recent assignment: Include the problem/challenge, what did you do to solve it, what was the outcome for the company, and a testimonial. This doesn't need to be done with professional graphics. It can be in an email or online-post format — sentences, bullet points, sentences. Share it online, send it via email to your network: "Who do you know with similar challenges? Please feel free to share." You also now gave them an easy way to introduce you.

Initially, don't worry about anything other than finding what works for you.

I was speaking with a business owner who had an incredible passion for sharing his story and helping other business owners discover the same enlightenment he has found. I suggested he reach out to his local chamber of commerce and industry associations. Find someone in programming and offer to speak. This could be a keynote, a lunch-and-learn, or as part of a panel. His first hurdle was, "How do I present myself to them?" In one week, he had several video clips to show his speaking abilities, a one-page bio to establish credibility, and a series of topics he could speak on. The video clips came from the two of us doing a podcast recording (a video meeting that was recorded). He picked out a couple of 2–3–minute segments and had someone clip the videos.

Once you find what works for you, consistency is key from two perspectives:

- Align it with your brand.
- Timing: Whether it is twice a week, weekly, or monthly, find a rhythm that works well for you, and consistently provide some type of insights or information on your expertise.

CHAPTER 9

Go-to-Market

The options for how to help companies alleviate the pain they are going through and achieve their vision, mission, and goals are only limited by our imagination and ability to execute.

There are various go-to-market strategies available. These strategies will depend on what you decided your expertise is, what type of work you enjoy doing, the problems you solve, and who has these problems.

Strategies

Here are a few examples of how to combine what you have discovered about what you like to do and are really good at, what problems you solve, and for whom you can solve them:

- An executive from the medical device industry knew the market, the competitors, the products, and how to market and sell to it. He decided, after decades of being on the road, that he didn't want to step in as an interim or fractional executive. Instead, he became an advisor for five companies in the industry and a related industry (noncompetitive), helping to align marketing and sales with the company's goals.

- An executive who had built two companies as a president and a CEO wanted to help other companies do the same. Though she'd had one successful exit, she decided to make sure her clients were fully committed to her. She worked with single-owner, privately held companies that were looking to sell in the next three years and needed help building enterprise value for the exit. She works with them initially on a project basis building a roadmap to create enterprise value. At the end of the project, they either commit to keeping her on as an advisor with a % of the exit, decide they can implement the roadmap without any external assistance, or decide not to increase the company's value. By the way, this is a great strategy for Ethan's brand, how he likes to solve problems, and the role he wants to play in the solution.

- An executive with years of experience in a single industry was looking for his next role after his company sold and the new CEO decided his skills did not align with the direction the company was going. He couldn't decide which sounded worse, going through a new job-search process or doing business development as an independent executive. He hadn't had high-profile leadership roles to leverage. He did have a lot of experience in an industry that was having problems finding good talent, getting the talent trained, and hiring experienced people to manage them. He decided to leverage his decades of experience and his networks to help solve some of these problems. He was able to connect with his network and find out who was struggling with this the most. He could identify emerging leaders in the organization, develop them for manager roles, and help them identify how to replace themselves as they were promoted.

- Rather than waiting for an opportunity for a role you want to be available, create the opportunity yourself. There is a growing trend for experienced or emerging growth-oriented executives to find potential acquisitions on behalf of financial sponsors and step in as the CEO or other executive role with some equity. Depending on the economic environment, financial sponsors, such as private equity or family offices, are looking for companies to invest in. Their challenge (or problem) is identifying these investment opportunities and getting the right leadership team to grow the investment post-acquisition. Some financial sponsors have made this part of their business development strategy: Find the CEO first, and the CEO finds the company(ies) to invest in.

- As an investor yourself or someone who wants to be careful about the next company/brand you join, working together on a project basis first may help you decide if this is a company and team you want to be part of longer term. It provides a lot of information and insights that may not be available otherwise, no matter how many interviews or how much due diligence you do.

- I could go on for a few more pages of examples. The possibilities are almost limitless — once you have clarity on what problems you want to solve. Having a strategy that aligns with these will shorten the path to conversations and increase the number of situations to which you want to say "yes."

People Who Know You

Sharing our brand and thought leadership with people we already know (and who know us) is a natural and easy start. We often miss this or haven't revisited it since we initially launched our business. We get caught up in "how many people we can meet this week," and we forget about those relationships we have spent years and decades establishing. Businesses end up in this trap, spending 95% of their marketing budget on origination business and 5% on nurturing clients and past clients.

One of the tough aspects for a longtime executive is narrowing down experience and establishing their brand. The good news is that your longtime executive career has done more for your network and adding to your "people you know" list than any amount of new networking you can do during the next year. Here's a start for your list:

- Anyone you have ever worked with. Play a game of, "Where are they now?" Type into your search engine their name and the company at which you worked with them. If you want to find them on a specific networking platform, type in the name of that, as well. (Re)Connect with them.
- Anyone you have gotten to know through volunteer work, especially nonprofit boards or your children's sports teams.
- Industry individuals you have met at various trade shows and golf tournaments.
- Anyone you have ever met networking who impressed you. They may not know your capabilities firsthand, but they have met you before.

- Past potential clients or direct-hire opportunities. Reach out to the head of HR or the hiring manager. Do they know you are available on a contract basis? You never know what the current situation is and how it may align with your expertise now that you have it clearly defined and easy to apply.
- Friends and family.
- Most importantly, past clients. They can also be a great referral source.

For any of your outreach, remember it is about them. Leading with you and your brand is one of the best ways to turn someone off. Even if you are sharing a piece of content you think they may be interested in, it is about the value it brings to them.

Using the list above for people you know:

- List them.
- Where are they now?
- Do they know you are available and the problems you solve? They know you. You may not even need to do much to convey your brand.

People Who Don't Know You Yet

Some people are able to say they have no need to meet anyone new in their life. Anyone who is looking to build a business is not one of those people. We are constantly going to be meeting new people, learning about them, and having them learn about us.

Leverage your years of experience as a leader, and create your own assessment. Is this someone who is a center of influence or with whom you enjoy collaborating? Are they a resource for you to refer to? Do you share an affinity? And so on.

Your assessment can be as simple as answering "yes" or "no" to a single question, or it could be a matrix you do in your head as you are meeting them. This can also help create some questions for you to ask when meeting new people. If meeting new people is difficult for you, think of it as an objective evaluation rather than an unpredictable social setting. Find what works for you.

"You only get one chance to make a good impression" holds true. Use your advisory board to role play. Record yourself, or practice in front of the mirror. Whether you are in person or virtual, how you come across matters.

Networking and Referral Guidelines

Networking doesn't necessarily mean going to every event we can fit on our calendars. Take the advice any of us would give a client: Be strategic. For example:

- Multiply your time by focusing on individuals who have multiple company introductions.
- Build a pool of resources for your clients and those who may never be clients but call you for a variety of recommendations.

- Bypass the trust and credibility phase of getting to know someone. Either they already know us, or we are being introduced by someone who has already established trust and credibility.

Here are some additional networking tips as you go-to-market with your product/service offering.

Choose Wisely

Choose events that either have a topic you are interested in, where someone invited you who can introduce you around, or that are likely to attract people who meet your criteria for "people I want to meet." The third is fairly obvious, but it can often be the least productive event without at least one of the first two criteria.

Ask Questions, and Be Curious

Being curious is one of my favorite strategies for getting to know someone. No one likes going to an event and being sold to, especially CEOs. Some don't even like going to events and meeting people. They go for the speaker, the topic, or because they were invited. Help put them at ease in a conversation. Ask questions, and get to know them. Whether they are potential referral resources or potential clients, you should end up knowing far more about them than they know about you.

It is very off-putting when I go to an event where someone knows nothing more than what my company does, and I am handed a business card with the comment, "If you ever need my services, please call me," and that is the extent of the conversation. You'd be surprised how often this happens. Many of our clients don't network, because they know most people they meet with either see them as a sales target or just tell them what they want to hear. That's not valuable to them. If you do meet potential clients, ask questions. Keep the conversation focused on them. If they can use your help, the conversation will turn into a discussion. Make a gentle offer, such as: "I'm happy to provide some advice once I know a little more. Let me know if you'd like to discuss further."

Rule of Three

A good rule of thumb a friend once gave me is: "If you connect with one person and schedule a follow-up meeting, then it was worth going. If you connect with three people and schedule follow-up meetings, leave the event, because it doesn't get any better than that." That's the Rule of Three. Beware of walking out with a handful of business cards and expecting results from just this one activity and a quick conversation. The purpose of going is to find individuals you want to have an extended conversation with. If you don't look forward to another discussion with them, then you may not want to count it toward your three. Whether it is one or three, create a system for follow-up, and be consistent with it.

Research

Do research on the speakers and panelists, especially if they happen to be C-level executives at companies that fit your target audience. The more you know about them, the more comfortable you will be having conversations with them after the event. Speakers always appreciate it when you come up to talk about them and what they said instead of what you want to sell them. An increased number of networking opportunities publish their list of attendees. Do similar research on them, including who may be a mutual connection.

Never Eat Alone

Another friend's rule when he's looking for work is: Never eat alone. He has every breakfast, lunch, and dinner scheduled. Basic math says that is 15 connections/reconnections per work week. The math can then be multiplied by the number of their connections. By implementing this strategy, combined with effectively communicating your brand and listening skills, you just multiplied your efforts exponentially.

Basic Manners

If you say you will do something, get it done right away, not a week later. This is part of your brand. This includes follow-up from a referral or introduction. Recognize the effort someone went through to make an introduction or to remember you for a referral. The general thought process is that if someone is too busy to say, "Thank you," they already have too much business. It also doesn't matter if the introduction or referral turned into something. It isn't about getting or not getting business; it is the fact that they thought of you (yay you!). I know someone who keeps a simple Excel spreadsheet with a few columns. The first column is "Referral

Received/Referral Given." It can include your workflow as a checklist across the columns or simply be a list of names. Find a way to keep track, and thank anyone who helps you.

Prioritize Your Contacts

When I joined a nationwide networking group, the ability to network was just short of 24/7. My options seemed limitless. I spent the first six months trying different strategies to figure out what worked for me. Once I figured out what worked best for meeting the people I wanted to meet, I then figured out with whom it made sense to keep in touch and with whom it made sense to leave it at the single conversation. After meeting hundreds of individuals, I have a list of about 25 with whom it makes sense to keep in touch. Some could refer me to a client, some I ended up referring to clients, and others I simply enjoy speaking with. Think of this as your 25 best friends list.

Your interactions with your "best friends" can include:

- Regularly scheduled meetings
- A quick email or phone call check-in (a calendar prompt is great)
- Sharing an article or event you think they may enjoy
- Commenting or reacting to something they have posted
- Inviting them to be part of your advisory board

The people on your list can also change over time based on your business or personal goals. Keep your interactions consistent with your brand, be memorable, be curious, and be authentic.

Stay Connected

If we try to keep in touch with everyone we have ever met on an ongoing basis, it quickly becomes challenging and gives us diminishing returns on our time. Leverage the tools available and ideas mentioned earlier to stay connected. Follow and respond to updates/posts from your connections. Send congratulations or endorsements, and use them as a reason to stay top-of-mind or to get together. Send out updates on what you are doing; even if people just see your name, you can stay top-of-mind. Today, social media is your publisher. Get your message out across all online platforms that make sense for you and your target audience. Even though most of your connections may not be potential clients, they may know people who might be. The more consistent you are with your brand, messaging, and publishing, the more you will stay top-of-mind for the right reasons. And stay in touch. There are limitless resources available for you to stay in touch with people. I have yet to have someone say, "Please don't share recent news or interesting articles with me." Even though they may not read them, doing this helps to keep you top-of-mind.

Be a Connector

When networking effectively with people you know and people you are getting to know, make finding out about them first a priority. I see conversations as treasure hunts. With whom can I help connect them so at least one, if not both, parties will find value. Helping others, whether they are your clients or your referral partners, is one of the most powerful elements of your brand you can build.

Tools of the Trade

Fortunately, technology and the availability of individuals with the expertise you need are available on a contract basis. Automate or outsource whatever you don't enjoy doing or is not within your skill set. Some common tools we know to be useful are:

- *CRM (customer relationship management)*: Think of this as your marketing and sales tool. This can help you:
  - Keep track of everyone you meet.
  - Know when you met them and what you discussed.
  - Set how often you want to follow up and send you a reminder.
  - Automate some of your communications.
- *Research*: You can recreate organizational charts, the most common roles a company is posting for (letting you know what their issues are), which companies are within your target parameters, who the contacts are at those companies, and so on. The more you know and can speak to it, the more opportunity you have to convey your brand to the right people in the right way.
- *Business Development Services*: I have yet to talk to an executive who says, "I can't wait to wake up each morning and call 150 business owners I don't know." There are individuals out there who have this skill set and

enjoy it. This isn't a strategy for everyone, but I have seen some do very well with it. Find a way to always be doing business development. Building your business is an investment in time and other resources.

These are not expensive strategies, but they do take an initial investment of time or money.

CHAPTER 10

Getting Alignment

U nderstanding why we want to help companies, what problems we solve, how we solve them, and what is unique about this combination is half the equation. The other half is the company that has the problem and needs help solving it. From this point forward, it's about what the company needs, not what we can solve. The more we understand what they are struggling with, the outcome they are looking for, and the impact of that outcome for them, the easier it is to connect the dots and find alignment, whether that is through us or another solution (in the form of a referral).

Discovery: Building a Partnership

People are always more comfortable selling something or someone other than themselves. It's human nature. Many people just aren't comfortable selling, period.

Fortunately, we are no longer trying to sell ourselves or our time. We are representing a brand that helps solve a company's problem. Once we understand a company's pain points and challenges, we can assess if it is within our area of expertise (aligned with our brand) or if it makes sense for us to refer to someone else. We'll cover the benefits of referring to someone else later.

For some executives, the discovery process is seamless and comes naturally. For many, however, it is neither seamless nor natural. It is a painful process that seems like it never goes anywhere or drags on forever. If you are in that group, I've put together some guidelines for you to pick and choose from, as you formulate your own process and style when assessing a company's needs and what solution set makes the most sense for them.

Think of it less as a process and more as building a partnership. In a survey, CEOs were asked, "When faced with a challenge or opportunity, what stops you from hiring a management consultant or interim executive?" The top response was, "Trust — believing they can do what they say they can do." When building a partnership, we need to establish credibility and reliability in order to create trust.

Practice reading people. Listen with your ears and eyes; ask the questions that are important to the client, and work to understand the pains they are having. If not, they likely will end up talking about something that is not really the issue. Whether you are a novice to these types of conversations or have been doing this most of your career, everyone has their own spin and techniques that work best for them. Here are a few suggestions:

- Listen carefully, and key in on what they are meaning to say, not just what they are actually saying.
- When answering their questions, again listen, and answer them directly rather than answering the question you want to answer.

- Stay on point, unless there is a compelling reason to talk about something else. If you want to guide the conversation to where you think the pain really is, guide with questions.

- Reiterate back to the client what you are hearing. Make sure you received the information as it was intended. Often, we use words and phrases they did not think of, and they start to have a eureka moment: "That's exactly it! I've been trying to figure out how to explain it."

- Make sure that if you tell a story, it is relevant. Tell a story about a client or past situation that is similar to this client's situation, and focus on how you resolved it with the team. If you do share, include a variety of company situations. I had an executive only share experiences from one company. The client saw it as only having one relevant experience.

- Listen twice as much as you talk.

- Be curious. Every discussion is an opportunity to learn about the company, the leadership, and the situation.

- Do your due diligence on the company. This will help get to the heart of the discussion sooner.

- Don't assume right away that you are the right fit for their needs. Any time an introduction is made, rather than saying, "I look forward to seeing how I can help you," I say, "I look forward to learning more about you, your company, your situation, and what you want to accomplish." Depending on what I know, I may leave the last part off. This shows I am going to listen and assess if I am the right fit or if I need to suggest another solution.

- When a company is in pain, it is easy to want a quick fix or to see the person helping as a superhero. Be careful not to overpromise.

We want to listen first, ask questions, and understand what the company is going through and where they want to go. Research is helpful to avoid asking the obvious questions and to have a basis of understanding prior to your talk. However, I have seen executives get to the first meeting with the client, and instead of listening, they immediately go into a monologue about how much they know about the client and the industry. The client is not impressed. The client wants to discuss how to grow their company to the next level, not how much you know about them, their company, and their industry. Often, this is the first time they are having this type of conversation, and they need an opportunity to brain dump.

Ethan and I practiced these conversations. Ethan knew how much work went into getting to the point of a discussion where he may be able to help. He'd had a few of these conversations in the past six months and knew how many different ways they could go. He wanted to be able to listen, digest the information, ask the appropriate questions, and help guide the discussion to action. When Ethan was introduced to a founder/CEO whose sales had stalled and who had a recent product launch that was not what he expected, he was ready for the discussion.

Ethan could tell by the email exchange that the CEO had a very short attention span. The meeting was scheduled for 45 minutes, and it was made clear that the CEO had a tight schedule. The CEO had never hired outside help and was nervous. The meeting ended up lasting more than two hours. The client was so engaged in the conversation that he pushed off his next two meetings. Ethan appreciated that the CEO valued his time, especially since he had driven an hour each way to be there. It was a seamless conversation. Ethan also used future-oriented language during the meeting, such as, "Next week, we can start working on what you just mentioned."

How an executive comes across to the client is extremely important. The initial conversation can make or break future meetings, even if you aren't meeting initially with the decision-maker. Although the person you are speaking with may not be making the decision, they often can influence it. The more natural and stimulating the conversation is, the more successful you will be.

Be aware of what you are saying and how it can be perceived. A simple comment of, "We can work on getting the sales team trained and the information documented, then zero in on what is causing the decreased sales ratio," can be taken as, "Once the sales team is trained and information is documented, your sales ratio will increase." It is easy to overpromise, whether it is intentional or unintentional. Set realistic expectations until you have all the information. Though you may be more than capable of delivering on it, there may be unknown roadblocks that exist.

Ethan leveraged his knack for simplifying information that tended to be difficult or esoteric. Again, from experience, he knew how many different directions the conversation could go, including never reaching a conclusion or sideways if he didn't manage the discussion. He created a list for himself of outcomes he wanted from the first discussion. He kept it as outcomes rather than a list of specific questions to be asked. This helped him guide the conversation without it coming across as a Q&A session. The client had the opportunity to open up to him, and Ethan then directed his questions within the context of what was important to the client.

Needs Assessment

Goals for the first meeting are to:

1. Determine if you are the right fit for what the client wants.
2. Determine if this is a client and/or engagement you want.
3. Understand the client's situation, what they need, what they are looking to accomplish, and what types of results they expect.
4. Get as much detail as you need, because you will use this information for your proposal/statement of work later, along with deliverables and timelines.

No. 3 is where most of the time is spent. A simple outline for this is:

- What isn't going well?
- What impact would this have on the business if it were going well?
- How will we know if it is going well?

For example:

- What isn't going well? Recent reduction in leads.
- What impact would this have on the business if it were going well? $1.2 million in revenue.
- How will we know if it is going well? Is this SMART (create a metric that is specific, measurable, attainable, realistic, and timely)? Initially, it could be as simple as identifying the leading indicator and setting an improvement goal once you have reviewed all relevant information.

Stay focused on the client's situation at all times, and begin thinking about how you might solve their issues. This approach turns the tables on CEOs. We have seen their entire demeanors change during meetings such as this. Clients appreciate when executives are truly interested in helping them solve their issues. Let the CEO do the talking, while you guide the conversation toward planning and solving rather than facts and statistics.

Be aware of the number of initial meetings the company asks of you and your upfront time investment. Depending on the size of the company and the engagement, you may need to have separate meetings with various stakeholders, either due to their availability or simply because it's part of their process. Be cautious of meeting with the same individual(s) more than two times, and ask yourself, "Are the meetings focused on information needed to scope the engagement, or have they strayed into actually beginning the engagement?"

Other Opportunities for Alignment

Our expertise may align perfectly with what the company needs. However, if we don't also have alignment on the following things, it may not be the right fit for either of you.

- **Budget**: Most of the time, your clients won't reveal (or know) their budget up front, but always ask. If they don't know it, ask how they will determine it. Do your best to understand what their thought processes are regarding budget, and keep this as part of the ongoing conversations until you get an answer.

- **Process**: Most clients do not have a process in mind for scoping a project and vetting an executive. They will appreciate talking it through with you, because this likely will be the first time they have thought about it. Details will include others they would like you to meet, who the decision-makers are, and who the influencers are (who will have input).
- **Timeline**: Most often, clients have a timeline in mind regarding when they would like to start. Find out about any potential delays in the process, such as vacations or conferences, that could hinder getting meetings scheduled. If they are unable to answer with a general timeframe, ask, "How soon do you want to get what we have discussed accomplished?" and work backward from there.

Once Ethan had all the information, he was careful to consider what was shared and the results of his inquiries. He had learned not to move on to asking for the business until he considered his discovery and analysis to determine if he even wants to ask for the business, or if there's a better option for the client (and him).

He remembered one of the executives, Anne, he had met at a recent roundtable. Anne has deep experience in the food and beverage industry and a smattering of experience in a few other industries. Her expertise is helping companies determine their go-to-market strategy, creating the plan, and implementing it. She has been a full-time employee her entire career. She ended up without a job when the company she was working for needed to make cuts. She saw this as a good opportunity to take some time with family and do self-care (all those appointments she had been putting off due to the demands and travel of her job). As she was taking this pause, she received referrals and introductions to companies with situations and problems she had previously solved. They each looked to hire her full time. Anne was enjoying her time off and not traveling three out of four weeks a month. She wanted to maintain some flexibility for the next couple of years.

Anne went through the initial discussions (a.k.a., interviews) with the perspective of understanding what the companies' issues were, what they were looking to achieve, and aligning them with the value she could bring. She did not sell herself. She kept the company in mind and showed her expertise through her questions and conversations. It is no surprise all three companies wanted to hire her. Since Anne is staying focused on what they are looking to achieve, she is confident she can help two of them achieve their outcomes on a part-time, fractional basis.

What about the third company? Anne can easily say, "No, thank you," and let them figure something out. This is disappointing for both the company and Anne, since she knows the direction they want to go in and knows her skill sets can help. Anne can advise the company, get them on the right path, and help them identify the right person to step in. With Anne as an ongoing advisor, the company has someone with expertise providing guidance and oversight, and Anne keeps the relationship. You don't know where this company will be one to two years from now, or what will happen with the other two companies Anne is helping. She is maintaining the relationship, doing what is in the best interest of the company, keeping her options open, and possibly even providing a full-time individual from her network — which has value, monetary or otherwise. We'll discuss some of these elements in more detail later.

Anne stuck out in Ethan's mind for two reasons:

1.   He wanted to get to the point where Anne was, having more opportunity than he could personally handle.

2.   As he got to know Anne, he listened, learned, and discovered where he complemented her expertise and where he overlapped it. He knew there was potential to either collaborate for a client or be a referral source for Anne.

We'll talk through some strategies of what an executive can do when there isn't clear alignment. As Anne showed, there are options other than "Yes" or "No, thank you" when we are focused on solving a company's problems.

CHAPTER 11

Getting to "Yes": Making the Ask

Since most of us don't come out of marketing and sales, this part doesn't come naturally either, or it is done in a high-pressure sales way that includes overpromising.

We understand that even with all the alignment that can exist, sometimes a client just isn't ready to move forward or have change happen. That's a book for another time. I recently had a client where we presented three candidates, all of whom could solve his problem. The list of why they weren't the right fit was extensive, including issues of geography and breadth of experience. Based on that feedback, I presented a candidate who lived 30 minutes from their location and had some form of experience in all aspects of the business. The client still found a reason for why it wasn't a good fit. We can only help people who are ready to be helped.

Narrowing Problems to Impact

For those who are ready, able, and willing, it is still a big decision. When a business is spending time or money, the leadership wants to know: How much time will it take, how much money will it cost, what will the outcomes be/will it solve my problem (impact to the business)? There is some correlation that often needs to happen to help connect the problems they see with the outcomes they want. For example, we may get a request for an operations expert to help hold the project managers accountable to get their jobs done on time and at the expected profit margin. The outcome is delivering job completion to their client on time and meeting the company's profitability goals. The problem may not be "project manager accountability." By digging in and asking questions, we may find the project managers don't have visibility to the costs on a daily/weekly basis (or at all). They are managing the numbers blindly. By this point in the process, we have our own hypothesis on what problems are causing the issues and can assess if they align with our skill set. We have a similar hypothesis of which ones will be most impactful to the client and can isolate which ones are the low-hanging fruit. The low-hanging fruit takes the least amount of time while moving the needle and gaining value for the client.

Another common pain point is not enough sales. Let's use the following as an example:

What problems are the company having, and which align with the ones you are best at solving?

- New leads are inconsistent
- No clear handoff from Marketing/Sales
- Sales rep turnover
- SEO ROI out of balance
- No sales KPIs
- Sales workflow isn't understood/followed
- We don't know what our value prop is anymore
- Lack of predictability in revenue
- Sales comp plan rewards the wrong behavior

As an expert, you likely have a checklist like this (or can create one) prior to any client discussion. Doing the preparation in advance allows you to stay more focused on what is being said — and not being said.

What problems are most impactful to the client?

- New leads are inconsistent
- No clear handoff from Marketing/Sales
- Sales rep turnover
- SEO ROI out of balance
- No sales KPIs
- Sales workflow isn't understood/followed
- We don't know what our value prop is anymore
- Lack of predictability in revenue
- Sales comp plan rewards the wrong behavior

This helps your questions stay around the impact of the problem, not just solving the problem. What does it mean to the company if the problem is solved? As the impact discussion occurs, your expertise will know where to start narrowing your list.

How do you isolate the problems to reduce the risk?

- New leads are inconsistent
- No clear handoff from Marketing/Sales
- Sales rep turnover
- SEO ROI out of balance
- No sales KPIs
- Sales workflow isn't understood/followed
- We don't know what our value prop is anymore
- Lack of predictability in revenue
- Sales comp plan rewards the wrong behavior

Rather than presenting a statement of work that will address the top 5–8 potential issues, start with the top 1–2 pain points. Lead with the ones that are simple, involve the fewest people, and can provide a lot of insight to some of the others.

A similar approach can be used when marketing your services. Divide up your most common deliverables into a smaller commitment for the client. Think through what value is gained by the company, and you can then productize your services.

Productization

It is always a fun challenge for any of us who are trying to productize a service. For clarification, I am using productization to describe a non-customized, homogeneous scope of work. This is a preset scope of work with the same problem statement, goal, set of activities to be performed, and deliverables. Go back to the list of steps that make up our services or how we solve problems. Some of these steps, especially the initial step, can be productized.

I was recently in a meeting with a group of CEOs. Here was the discussion:

- **CEO 1**: "I am not happy with my finance person."
- **CEO 2**: "I went through a couple of finance people until I got connected with this fractional CFO service. They got my accounts cleaned up and are now closing out the books and preparing my financials for $X per month."
- **CEO 1**: "Sold. Send me their information."

What does a productized statement of work look like for the problem described in this discussion?

Problem Statement: Company's financials are not accurate, being completed in a timely manner, or being presented in an understandable or actionable way.

Goal: Have accurate and timely financial statements each month (can also include by a specific date of the month).

Activities:

- Understand business drivers, revenues, COGS, expenses.

- Review and reorganize chart of accounts as needed.

- Reconcile and adjust accounts — may be spread over X# of months based on initial review.

- Create a financial package that can be used to make informed decisions for the business.

Deliverables:

- Accurate, timely financial statements on a monthly basis.

Cost: $X per month

Being an expert and branding yourself for the type of problems you have solved many times before makes it much easier to separate your activities and deliverables into easy-to-communicate, understand, and move-forward pieces.

Productization can also help isolate value. The value you bring is decades of experience, not the 100 hours to accomplish the outcome. Your experience and process help companies avoid mistakes and wasted time, and it gets them to the solution quicker.

I know someone who figured out how to solve an issue that used to take a number of resources and downtime totaling $100,000 over a couple of months. After doing this time after time for years, he figured out how to do it in two hours by himself, and he charged $10,000. He does a couple of these a month, in addition to the rest of the work he does for his clients.

Though this seems extreme, the same concept is applied to sales trainings, coaching, and group sessions. Since most independent executives are not pricing through productization, I will discuss some other pricing strategies to determine what to charge for your services. When the company isn't clear on the value and outcome of what you can do, the uncertainty greatly affects what a company is willing to pay.

Product idea for past clients

Sherie has been working as an interim COO for the past 9 months at a small yet fast-growing company. After a couple of starts and stops, they finally found a direct-hire director of operations, allowing less dependency on the interim COO. As Sherie transitions them to the longer-term solution, she has a couple of options:

- Continue to work inside the company alongside the new director of operations for as long and as much work as she can get. Hint: It won't take long for the owner to question the cost of having both the direct hire and Sherie. When the client brings it up first, the interim executive has already overstayed their welcome and value.
- Find a date when the transition will be final, and Sherie moves on to her next assignment and set of business-development activities. She can check in with everyone occasionally to see how things are going.
- Sherie can put together a leadership insurance policy for her client. This can be everything from continuing to run the weekly team meeting one hour a week, to regular coaching check-ins with the new director of operations, to being an advisor to the owner as needed, to a

scheduled quarterly meeting with the owner and additional leadership. This is a low-cost investment for the client to help ensure that what Sherie started either continues or gets improved on, especially as the company grows and needs to shift.

The Rate

I have published a lot of information over the years about various formulas and calculations to figure out what rate to charge. Here's some modified guidance to help strike a balance between your goals and what makes sense for the client. First, talk to others doing similar or relatable work, and survey what they are charging and in what situations. A few factors to consider when you are deciding what to charge:

- Your availability, your financial situation, and your Why: If you like to keep busy and simply want to help companies, you may charge $75 per hour. If you have a certain amount you need to make each month, you may charge $150 per hour. I know some executives who have turned down $100 per hour and have gone without any client work for months rather than take a rate below what they want. It is a personal decision for you and your business.
- Value to the client: Are you helping them increase the value of their company by millions, or are you solving a problem that is being required by their client and doing nothing but costing them money, including your services that are estimated at $50,000?

- Time commitment: Will you be spending 8 hours a month, 8 hours a week, or 5 days a week? The less time spent each month tends to be at the upper end of your rate range.

- Did you source the client, your investment in that client so far, what will it take to service the client? Some clients simply take up more time and energy than others. Some come through referral sources that have you starting within a week, and they are managing the relationship, contracts, and invoicing.

Reduce the Risk

Reduce the risk for the client with clarity on how long it will take, how much it will cost, and what problems will be solved. Add expected outcomes if they are known and realistic. For example: "Give me 60 days to put in place a comp plan that will reward the behaviors we want (notice the "we") and the KPIs to monitor the progress. It will take an estimated # of hours/days per week at X rate."

The theme throughout the book has been to make it easy. Make it easy for people to understand what problems we solve and how we help companies. Make it easy for people to remember us. Make it easy for prospective clients to trust us. Make it easy for them to take the chance and move forward on your solution for them. Remember, they have the option to move forward with anyone who can solve their problem. Make it easy for them to say "yes" to your solution.

Pro Bono Work

I brought up Bob earlier in the book. He grew and sold his own company, then did the same for his friend's company. Financially, he doesn't need to continue to work. He is driven to help other business owners avoid the same mistakes he made and to help develop the next generation of leaders. Being in the position to do it for free doesn't mean he should. The question is how Bob's clients value his services if nothing is being paid for them. Having some investment in the process and the value Bob is providing sometimes is an important part of the development.

Where pro bono could make sense is in gaining experience you don't have already. I had an experienced teacher referred to me for career advice. She wanted to switch careers to marketing. She had no experience in marketing but felt she would be really good at it. I connected her with the CEO of a nonprofit education organization. I suggested she do a marketing project that would be meaningful to this nonprofit. Since she already has the expertise in education, she could invest her time in developing experience in a new area leveraging a known area. In exchange, the nonprofit CEO will provide a testimonial, and she can add the experience to her online footprint.

The Lifecycle of an Engagement

As is the case in life, a career, or the growth of a company, an independent executive engagement is not a straight line. There are various situations that cause ups and downs:

- What the company shares during discovery doesn't always align with reality once the engagement starts. The company needs more assistance than they initially thought.

- Due to the urgency of the situation and outcomes, more work needs to be done up front, then it will taper off as the infrastructure is put in place.

- The first couple of weeks may be dedicated to an assessment that will not take as much consistent time. What the company needs, and the type of engagement they need, may not be clear until an initial assessment is done, and the company determines where the executive can provide the most value.

- Even though an independent executive does not need oversight or onboarding, they do need information that can sometimes be constricted or bottlenecked by availability of internal resources. It could take a couple of weeks of stop, go, and wait to get enough information to take action. The smaller the team, the longer it takes to get to the heart of what needs to be done.

- The company's cash flow may be a constraint, which is why the executive is being brought in. I placed a fractional CFO into a small company that had the cash flow for 10 hours a month. The fractional CFO worked with the company 10 hours a month for about four months until he was able to put the picture together and give the CEO better visibility to cash flow and projections, and identify some operational cost savings. Within a year, the fractional CFO was working with the company 10–20 hours a week, depending on the season.

- The dependency on the independent executive decreases over time, as the goals and outcomes are achieved, and longer-term solutions are put in place. There is a ramp-down period and, possibly, an ongoing advisory role to help ensure stability and growth.

There does need to be some flexibility in scheduling and availability on behalf of the independent executive and, sometimes, the company. The more this is discussed up front and ongoing, the more the expectations will be clear for everyone involved, and potential conflicts will be avoided.

It can be challenging to determine availability needed, especially when there is M&A activity involved. For these situations, consider a percentage-of-time engagement. For example, I have placed fractional CFOs who support business plans, fundraising, and M&A activities. It is unknown weeks in advance if there will be a week where four days will be needed for a couple of weeks and only one day for a period of time. We talk this through with the company and find a percentage of time the independent executive will reserve for the client. This is done as a monthly retainer. Understanding that all the time may not be used in a given month and the executive can repurpose it toward other activities or clients that week, the independent executive gives a discounted rate when doing a monthly retainer. It ends up being a win-win for both the executive and the company that gets the expertise needed without a full-time, longer-term commitment.

Pulling It All Together

1. Create your independent executive business plan.
   a. Determine Why you want to help people and businesses.
   b. What are you great at?
   c. What value do you bring?
   d. What problems do you solve?
   e. For whom do you solve them?
2. Determine what type of independent executive business model works best for you and your services.
3. Be clear, consistent, and memorable with your messaging.
4. Be the expert; be a thought leader.
5. Create a strategy for your go-to-market starting with people you know and, more importantly, who know you and the value you bring.
6. When speaking with someone you can help, it's about them, their pains, and where they want to go.
7. Make it easy for a potential client by minimizing the risk of working with you and maximizing the impact of what you can do.

CHAPTER 12

Diversify Your Portfolio

Ethan did the work and gained the clarity needed to go from nonstop activity with little to no results to being a known solution provider within his network and beyond. Knowing Why he wanted to help companies helped him refine what problems he solved and how he was helping them. This clarity ignited a fire in all his communications, networking, and discussions with both potential referral partners and clients. Ethan could see how to leverage his decades of experience and connections into a business.

As you develop your business into whatever you want to make it (a sustainable business, a lifestyle, a transition), here is an overview of what it may look like. The three components I have seen affect an executive's decision-making about what works best for them are:

- Time commitment
- Number of clients you like to have concurrently
- Amount of business-development (BD) effort

Engagement Type	Time Commitment	Number of Clients	BD Effort
Coaching, Advisory, Boards	<8 hours/month 6–12+ months	5–10	Medium
Consulting, Project-Based	Variable	1–3	Low–High
Interim	3–5 days/week 3–9 months	1–2	Medium–High
Fractional	1–2 days/week Years	2–5	Low
Direct Hire	All	1	Highest

Here are some examples of engagement type from an executive's perspective:

Advisory: I have worked with an executive who has an incredible aptitude for reading and understanding the triggers in a business. He can influence teams through discussions, not title or authority. He can help a business owner understand the numbers, the people, and the best path forward, then guide them there. The thought of stepping in to manage any part of the business on a part-time instead of a full-time basis doesn't make any sense to him. He doesn't see how he would be able to do it with the way he manages things. This is common for individuals who have been CEOs and make great advisors. They either want to advise the CEO or be the CEO of the company hands-on, full time.

Fractional is an attractive option for those who can juggle multiple situations at one time and enjoy a consistent client base with less business development. Fractional lends itself to growing businesses that don't have a full-time need, but the need is ongoing at this point. There likely is some heavy lifting to be done initially, but once stabilized, the executive helps build on that and supports the growth of the company and, hopefully, the surrounding leadership.

Interim is usually preferred by those looking to step in and engage themselves with one, maximum two, clients at a time. It does have the biggest highs and lows with regard to scheduling, which works best for some. You may take on an interim assignment that consumes you for 6–9 months, then take a couple of months to travel, spend time with family, or focus on having three meals a day.

Consulting, Project-Based: I have not touched on this much since this tends to be blended into interim or is used to describe larger-scale, multiperson projects. It can be anything from three people bidding on a one-year project with a Fortune 100; to a series of small projects, such as assessments and building some SOPs; to supplemental help for a past client.

Be clear on which you want to do and are brought in to do. This will help you when balancing your workload and what you want to say "yes" or "no" to. Doing two interim assignments as a quarterback would be a lot.

Over the years, I have seen just about every combination of executive careers. Hopefully this book has provided some guidance for being more purposeful. The more information we can all share, the more we can help each other achieve our goals. How we help them isn't always a straight line.

The above gives you an idea of what one type of contract work looks like vs. another; it doesn't mean that is the only thing you may do. Over time, you will likely end up with a career looking more like a portfolio of business and clients. Think of Sherie, who was an interim COO for nine months and then transitioned to an advisory role with monthly and quarterly check-ins.

Engagement Type	Portfolio 1	Portfolio 2	Portfolio 3
Coaching, Advisory, Boards	1-2	2+	5+
Consulting, Project-Based	1	1 (at a time)	supplemental
Interim	1		supplemental
Fractional		2-3	

You can stay diversified even in a direct-hire, full-time role. It is not uncommon for executives employed by one company to also serve on boards. The executive may also have a few advisory or coaching clients. This provides the executive with ongoing development and insights from outside the company or industry. The employer often benefits from this in many ways.

Creating a Feedback Loop

Over time, you can see how one feeds into the other, and the need for business development or job interviewing gets reduced. The more meaningful interactions you have, the more opportunities you'll have to work with people in different ways. They are able to not just understand your brand, but also experience your brand and become a brand ambassador.

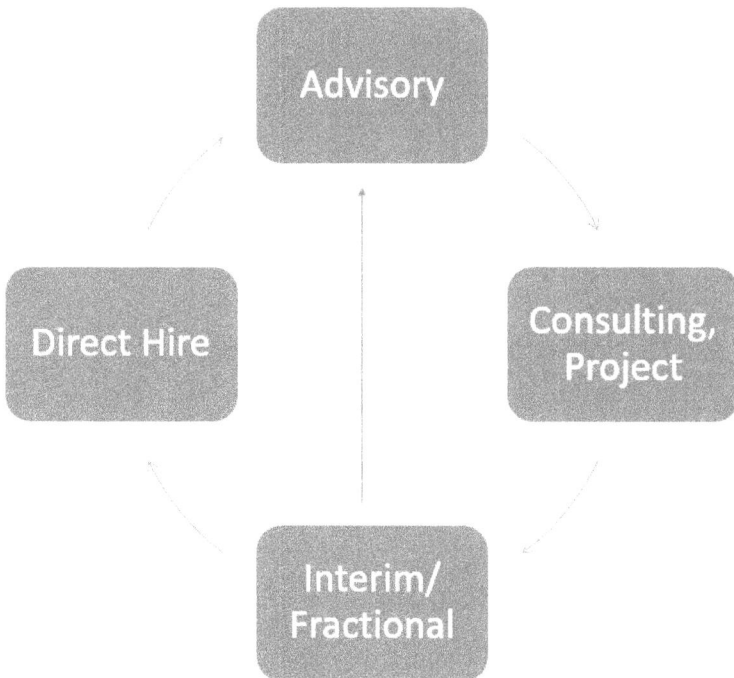

CHAPTER 13

Multiply Your Revenue Streams

As Ethan's reputation, opportunities, and business grew, he could see it evolving beyond a business of one. Since he was now looking at his efforts as a business, he was recognizing all the value he was providing to his clients, networks, and others — and not charging for it. He knew there were additional avenues to expand what he had built into a multi-revenue platform.

Revenue Channels

The best business plans have multiple revenue streams. An executive's business is no different. There are opportunities to create revenue streams leveraging principles from this book. The most common are:

- Doing the work yourself
- Thought leadership works for you 24/7
- Referrals

Doing the Work Yourself

I won't spend much effort going into this, since it has been covered extensively. This can be the only revenue stream or the platform for additional revenue streams.

Thought Leadership

There is an opportunity to monetize your expertise in the form of models, checklists, guides, trainings, books, and so on. It may not be a large revenue stream, but it can pay big dividends in terms of additional marketing and outreach opportunities.

Referrals and Referral Fees

Never pass up an opportunity to make a referral. Even if you decide to not have it affect you monetarily, it affects your relationship bank account. This can never be underestimated and will pay dividends in many ways.

I am often asked my opinion on referral fees. I am going to speak to the talent market only (not referring to a CPA or attorney) and say each situation is different, and there is an investment we have all made in building our networks and relationships over time. I do believe there is a value in that.

Types of Referrals

There is a difference in types of referrals:

Scenario 1

John is referring someone to me who has a business challenge. After some discussion, I determine I am not the right solution for them, but Sally is a great fit. I am happy to make an introduction directly to Sally or ask John if he would like to speak with Sally first and make the introduction himself.

Scenario 2

Terry is an interim CFO. She gets a call from a potential client she spent some time with earlier this year. They decided not to move forward with the acquisition and didn't need her help. They just had their controller quit and are checking to see if Terry can step in. Terry prefers M&A work and is not that excited about reconciling accounts and closing out the books. She has gotten to know a few people who could be a good fit for this. She contacts each of them to see if they are available and talk through the opportunity. Terry invested time getting to know the client and building a network of executives who may be a good fit. Terry can arrange with the individual(s) she is introducing for a referral fee in the event the client decides to move forward with them. Whether Terry decides to set up a referral fee arrangement or not, it is a good opportunity to do a few check-ins with the client to see how the engagement is going and if they need any other support.

Scenario 3

Leonardo is an operations consultant who gets a call from a client he worked with last year. They have a supply chain issue and need Leonardo to step in and assist. Unfortunately, Leonardo is tied up on another interim assignment and can't dedicate the time needed. Leonardo has gotten to know others who can solve such problems. He hasn't worked with any of them directly and wants to make sure things go smoothly. Leonardo is already set up with the client and is a trusted resource. He can manage the billing through his own company and act as project manager. Another option is for the interim to bill directly to the client with Leonardo staying involved as an advisor to ensure the engagement goes as smoothly as possible. Leonardo can adjust his referral fee based on his involvement level.

Leonardo could have seen each of these individuals as competitors, referral sources, or potential revenue opportunities. Ethan saw it similarly with Anne. Since he and Anne had some overlap of expertise, he could have seen her as a competitor and let that be the last discussion they had. Instead, he developed it into future discussions, shared thought leadership with Anne, and eventually got the opportunity to work with Anne and a client of hers. It was such a great experience for the client, Ethan, and Anne, that they wrote up a case study on it, along with a testimonial. The case study read like a mystery novel with Ethan and Anne as the detectives. It is always great when you can find a way to entertain as well as educate. Their collaboration was the icing on the cake.

When meeting people, especially those in our industry who are seemingly competitors, be curious and get to know them. There are opportunities for us all to be the relationship manager, the one doing the work, or the one providing the talent referral. In the end, it takes a village to help a business grow. Find your village, and be a resource at every opportunity.

Types of Partnerships

There are various levels of referral relationships:

Referral Partnership

- Can be pro bono or, if it makes sense, for a referral fee.
- If you decide to set up a referral fee arrangement, it can be a handshake or a written agreement.
- Revenue or no revenue, it creates good will and stickiness.

Connections, introductions, and referrals are what my world revolves around. I connect people for a living. It is in my blood. Those connections range from people who have similar affinities to individuals who may be able to do commerce together. As unintuitive as it seems, I tend to have stronger referral relationships with individuals and firms who could be considered competitors.

I provide interim and fractional executive services. I receive referrals from firms that provide interim and fractional CFO services. The firm receives a request from a former client with a need no one in their firm has the capacity for or lacks the ability to be onsite; they contact me, and my company supports that specific client situation. It is still their client, whether I am working through the referral partner or directly with the client. Rather than saying, "We can't help," the referral partner has solved the client's issue, we loop them in for any other client needs, they have a substantial reason to keep in touch with the client, and they have an additional line item on their income statement from the referral fee.

Strategic Partnership

- Create additional bandwidth for yourself or complementary expertise. Example: A supply chain expert likely has a strategic partnership with an ERP implementor.
- Thought leadership collaboration (webinars, podcast, co-author).
- Content share: tag, interview, quote (sharing each other's networks).

As the market continues to segment itself from an expertise perspective, as well as consolidate resources for single-solution providers, a strategic partnership is a great way to grow your pipeline with opportunities aligned to your expertise while providing an expanded range of services.

Anne is a great example of how this can be done. Anne can focus on what she loves — go-to-market strategy in the food and beverage industry — while also helping companies through the planning and execution stages. She can create a strategic partnership with individuals who may also bring her in for opportunities that align best with her skill sets. Since there is clarity on their expertise, the industry, and the type of issues they solve, the content they can produce together is almost limitless. They will be the first phone call when the need arises.

Business Partnership

- One brand
- Shared resources
- Shared revenue

This is an option when there is proven alignment and the opportunity to create synergies. With shared resources, marketing and business development services may make more sense. This works best when there is productization and the workload (and revenue) is evenly shared. For example, leadership training services. This can be a consistent statement of work and shared responsibilities. They could be divided by industry expertise or elements of the trainings. One person may be best at one-to-one coaching, while the other is great at the group trainings. If one person is good at finding the business, the revenue share can accommodate for business origination.

Just as there are multiple scenarios to which a company can apply an executive's expertise, there are multiple ways an executive can leverage their network.

When you receive an email, direct or mass distribution, about a job or engagement opportunity, you have three choices:

1. Quickly determine it doesn't fit your skills or what you want, hit "reply," and ask the sender to stop sending you opportunities that aren't a good fit for you.
2. Review the email, determine if it isn't a good fit or what you want, and

hit delete.

3. Review the email and immediately start processing your skills and anyone else you can think of against the information provided. If it isn't a good fit for you, you hit "forward," and start sharing it with others who may be a good fit.

I have experienced them all from the receiving end. I highly recommend No. 3. One of the greatest connectors I know reads every opportunity email she gets from every organization she belongs to and spends about 30 minutes each week forwarding them to people she thinks should know about them. You can imagine what her relationship bank account looks like.

CHAPTER 14

Always be Prepared

It took Ethan a couple of years to build his independent business to the point of being a thought leader. He went from building his center of influence list to being on everyone else's. He gets to decide what he works on and who he works with. He has built a strong network and great partnerships to which to refer everything else. The only regret he had was not being more prepared and having a plan for "what if" or "someday."

Some executives are not prepared to be independent. They have mostly worked with established or fully supported companies. They have been surrounded by a team, and they have had a clear focus on what the company does and the marketplace where they are selling, or they get to focus on one key area of the business. Now they need to work as a solopreneur. This can be a difficult shift to make.

There are various factors to think through when transitioning to being independent for the first time. Similar factors should be considered when accepting a direct-hire role after being independent. Some differences include:

- **Infrastructure**: Are you used to a large company with lots of support and infrastructure or a smaller company where you are doing everything yourself? For example, when your computer isn't working, are you OK finding a vendor to fix it or sitting online with customer support for half the day? With today's technology and availability of virtual assistants, this is easily overcome.

- **Business development**: Your income is directly related to the amount of time you invest and your ability to develop your own business.

- **Being a business of one**: As human beings, we are herd animals. We enjoy being around, working with, and engaging with other human beings. Being a business of one can be more challenging than we expect. If this is not a challenge for you, and you really enjoy being a business of one, do some reflection on the business development bullet point. It is going to be a teeter-totter.

The more time you have to plan and prepare, the more purposeful and intentional you can be. Recently, I had two separate CEOs (not business owners) ask me about being independent executives. They each believe they have a two-to-three–year horizon left in their CEO role. Now is the perfect time for them to start preparing in the following ways:

- **Build your net**: Get involved in your industry associations, preferably on a committee or informal board/advisory council. This includes functional or affinity-based associations, such as finance- or HR-focused organizations. The bigger and stronger the net you build, the easier it is to take that leap when the time comes.

- **Build your communication skills**: This is the No. 1 differentiator I see with executives. The ability to communicate their brand and what they can do is critical. Find a coach, join an organization that focuses on two-way communication (not just public speaking), get feedback, and work on it.

- **Build your war chest**: I heard this term in a CEO peer group. The concept was about storing up liquid reserves in the event of a downturn or to leverage an opportunity. The more intentional we are about the possible directions we may want to take, the more prepared we are mentally and financially, which opens more options for our career choices. With financial reserves, you have the option to take the roles (interim, fractional, direct hire, etc.) that fit your value proposition and that you enjoy. You can focus on what the company needs rather than the financial pressures of a personal situation.

- **Build your advisor base**: This can be in the form of advising one-to-one, an advisory board, or a board of directors. This will help build your network and your experience. If you are a sitting executive, it helps you develop the ability to create change through influence rather than the title of your current role. Let your network know you are open to board roles. The shortest route to being on a board is when you are currently in a sitting executive role. It looks good for you and the company.

- **Build your brand**: Regardless of your work arrangement, your title, or your work type, your brand is one of the few things you will carry with you throughout your career. It may evolve over time, but this is the foundation of what you enjoy, what you can do, and your value to others.

Being independent means starting a business. Even if it is seen as a bridge to the next role, it is a business. It has a brand, a story, messaging, and infrastructure. The independent executive is now responsible for business development, marketing, sales, IT, operations, accounting, and finance. Depending on your background, some of these are part of your expertise, while others can be scary or simply annoying. After listening to thousands of executives for more than 15 years, there is no question the most challenging responsibility is business development.

This includes developing a portfolio of clients. I used to quote a timeline for what it takes to build a sustainable pipeline of business. I now see it as a product of multiple factors, including your ability to communicate effectively, the extent of your engaged network, how selective you are with the type of work you do, the rate you charge, and the effort you put into it. Some people have a full schedule within months, while others struggle for years.

The shortest path to building an independent business is being intentional, being prepared, and creating a plan. Regardless of where you are in your journey, by leveraging the concepts discussed here, you can create a roadmap that helps you get to where you want to be with your career.

Pulling It All Together

1. Create a portfolio of clients over time where you can support them in various ways throughout their lifecycle.
2. There are multiple avenues for creating value from your expertise and background. You can create additional revenue streams beyond your core business.
3. You never know what is ahead. The more prepared you are, the more options you have, and the better chance you have for success, however you define that.

Final Thought: A Community of Leaders

I'd love to create a world where there is no need for anyone to submit a job application or create a job post. We can create an ecosystem where we are two degrees away from anyone we need in order to achieve our goals. I do believe that connections make the world move forward and become a better place. Whether you are someone who exists to help and serve others to achieve their goals, or you need to build an army around you to achieve your own goals, we can achieve both through a community of leaders helping to build it.

For more resources or to be part of a community of leaders, you can learn more at **Thesolutionexecutive.com**.

About the Author

Kristen McAlister has spent most of her career helping companies create value and grow. She has spent the past 15 years teaching companies how to leverage leadership and build teams to support growth.

She is a speaker and multi-book author on topics including leadership teams, talent management, contingent workforce, and independent executive careers. Kristen is a mother, Ironman, and retired Marine wife.

www.ingramcontent.com/pod-product-compliance
Lightning Source LLC
Chambersburg PA
CBHW060619210326
41520CB00010B/1393